I0814512

Memorial Coliseum

75 Years as Monument, Stage, and Arena

Kevin Cook

Foreword by Jim Host

P.O. Box 238
Morley, MO 63767
(573) 472-9800
www.acclaimpress.com

Cover design: Frene Melton
Cover photo: Bob Willcutt
Layout: Steward & Wise Design

ISBN: 978-1-938905-58-2 | 1-938905-58-X
Library of Congress Control Number: 2024945157

First Print: 2025
Printed in the United States of America
10 9 8 7 6 5 4 3 2 1

Contents

Foreword

I first experienced Memorial Coliseum on December 23, 1953, when UK men's basketball was playing LaSalle for the UKIT championship. UK won, 73-60, over the team that ended up winning the NCAA championship. Kentucky finished undefeated that year. The NCAA declared Cliff Hagan, Frank Ramsey, and Lou Tsioropoulos ineligible for the NCAA Tournament because they were fifth-year players (they would be eligible today). Hagan scored twenty-eight in that game on his way to an All-American season. Tom Gola scored eighteen and went on to be LaSalle's leading scorer and was Most Outstanding Player in winning the NCAA title in 1954. The building was awesome because I had never seen any building like it. I had grown up in Ashland and listened to every UK game as announced by Claude Sullivan on the Standard Oil Network.

The next time I was in the building was when I signed a full athletic scholarship in baseball. I got my locker in the Coliseum where the baseball team dressed, went out on the basketball floor, and looked up to the seats where my dad and I had sat. I could not believe how big and bright it was. Baseball played across the street at the end of Stoll Field, where the UK football team also played. We would run and work out on the Coliseum concourses during the wintertime. Sometimes Coach Rupp would send a manager up to quiet us down.

I did play-by-play for the UK student radio station on the Coliseum's press row, did the Kentucky high school tournament from the same site, and saw many games while sitting beside Cawood Ledford and Ralph Hacker during UK home games.

It does not seem possible that what at one time was the largest arena on a college campus is now seventy-five years old. This book as done by Kevin Cook is a terrific history of what this great building has meant to the University of Kentucky, as well as to the people of the Commonwealth in remembrance of the names of those Kentuckians who gave their lives fighting for the freedom we all have in this country.

Jim Host, UK class of '59
(My degree says '61 because it took two additional years for me to pass Spanish.)

DEDICATION

This book is dedicated to the Kentucky men and women of the United States Armed Forces who sacrificed their lives for their fellow Americans, blessing them with a free and hopeful nation. May we always remember why the Coliseum proudly bears the name "Memorial."

Acknowledgments

Many kind people have contributed to this work, and I cannot offer enough appreciation for their liberal help in so many ways and forms. I wish to thank first my father, E. Dean Cook, for teaching me love of country and UK basketball; and my mother, Ruth Cook, for sharing with me her love of reading. Above all, both of them demonstrated to me the unfailing love of God. My brothers, Scott, Todd, and Jon, have been life-long friends and supporters of my writing. My wife, Elke, and children, Katie and Jacob, have been lovingly and inspiringly beside me through the long process of putting this book together.

Doug Brunk, a prolific and talented writer on UK sports history, has been an invaluable sounding board for me for many years, and his encouragement is what got me into the writing business. Jim Host was kind enough to read my previous book and offer a supportive critique. He then generously helped to connect me with Acclaim Press for this project. Lieutenant Colonel (retired) Allen Back of the UK Army ROTC battalion provided significant guidance on identifying and discussing the military-oriented sites and markers across the UK campus. His unit, as well as the UK Air Force ROTC program, continue to carry the flame of honorable military service at the University. I extend much gratitude to each of the persons who graciously shared their personal memories of Memorial Coliseum, which appear in a chapter inside where you will find their names. Jason Flahardy, the photographic archivist of UK's Special Collections Research Center, steered me through the legal process that granted me permission to reproduce many of the book's images. Stacey McChord of RossTarrant Architects went out of her way to put me in contact with persons who could assist me with my questions about the renovation's architectural process. Tony Neely, an assistant athletic director for athletics communication and public relations, was very helpful as I pursued permission to reproduce architectural concept drawings of the completed renovation. Ben Godwin and Randy Coole of Catapult led me through the final steps of acquiring permission to reproduce those amazing architectural images here. Architect Royce Bourne sat down with me to examine the concept of my manuscript as a whole from an architect's perspective, and also offered insightful views on the original design of the Coliseum. Mike Harreld, former team manager for Coach Rupp, provided a gold mine of inside information on Kentucky's practice routine. UK Hall of Famer Dennis Emery, former tennis coach for the Wildcats, kindly gave me access to the image of John McEnroe playing Jim Courier in the Coliseum, a match that Emery organized and promoted. Cole Combs discussed structural changes related to the Coliseum's renovation. Joel Vincent, secretary of the Committee of 101, took the time to put me in touch with veteran members Rex Payne, Buddy Rosenberger, and Gene Oakley, all of whom helped me to better understand this important organization. Finally, many thanks to Acclaim Press Publisher Doug Sikes, who believed in my "pitch" for a book on Memorial Coliseum, and Randy Baumgardner, my editor at Acclaim, who walked me through the many finishing steps for this volume with the assurance of an experienced pro.

Introduction

On a summer afternoon in August of 2022, a public memorial service to celebrate the life of Mike Pratt was held inside Memorial Coliseum on the campus of the University of Kentucky. A beloved figure within Kentucky sports and far beyond, Pratt had recently passed away. Among other accomplishments in his eventful life, Pratt had recently completed his twentieth year as color commentator on the UK men's basketball radio network, a team that he had played for as a collegiate star over five decades before. The ceremony included a minister's homily, eulogies from friends and family, the playing of poignant music, and an audio replay from Pratt's final UK home game in that same hall. The choice of Memorial Coliseum for the observance was appropriate, for it encompassed everything the arena was designed to be for the Commonwealth of Kentucky: a place to collectively and reverently honor those who have passed on, to hear meaningful words and music, and to gather together the state-wide basketball kinship known as the Big Blue Nation.

The origins of the Coliseum, however, started with UK's overwhelming need to accommodate more basketball enthusiasts in the stands, with no consideration given to its being a war memorial or public auditorium. When a field house facility was first proposed in the 1930s to succeed UK's Alumni Gymnasium, then only a decade old, it was to accommodate the already swollen crowds trying to cram onto bleachers meant to hold only a few thousand fans. Adolph Rupp's Wildcats were winning big and it seemed that everyone on campus and in town wanted to see the action. Alumni Gym

The front of the Coliseum prior to its renovation.

had been assumed to be more than spacious enough when it opened to great fanfare in 1924, but that was before the basketball team's performance began to improve greatly and Rupp had taken over the program in 1930. Soon, the "Baron" had elevated his squad to national prominence, and rabid followers without a ticket were relegated to standing room on the gym's sidelines or were even turned away at the doors. To take advantage of greater gate revenues from bigger crowds, Rupp increasingly took his squad to larger venues, playing in Louisville, Chicago, New Orleans, and New York City. As the years passed, Kentucky was playing fewer games at their own arena, limiting the opportunity of local fans to see their beloved Wildcats play.

The University's first response to the exploding popularity of Kentucky basketball was to propose a field house, a multipurpose building expansive enough for indoor football practice as well as a basketball court surrounded by perhaps 6,000 seats. Offices and even dorm rooms were to be accommodated within the design. But the perennially underfunded school's finances were exacerbated by the Great Depression, and every idea put forth for such a facility inevitably fell through for lack of money within the institutional and state budgets. Additionally, Frank McVey, the UK president, was not a champion of intercollegiate sports and was adamant that his school not go into debt for a field house, especially when there remained many needs for academic and dormitory infrastructures.

It was not until 1941, when new University president Herman Donovan was inaugurated, that the push for a field house was revived. This time the president lobbied the Kentucky legislature to fund a building that would benefit not only the campus, but the community as well. The government in Frankfort was willing. It was now to be a field house—auditorium, where concerts and civic events could be held as well as basketball games. The amenities and price tag would go up, but as a showpiece public building its value to Kentucky's citizens would also greatly increase. World War II, however, soon interrupted any thoughts of funding public structures when the nation

The floor of the Coliseum before its renovation.

needed ships, airplanes, and tanks. The University patiently waited for the end of the great crisis when it fully expected to break ground on the field house–auditorium. In the meantime, it was mutually agreed that the building, when ultimately erected, would also serve as a memorial to the citizens of Kentucky who had died for their country in the global conflict. (As a precedent, Memorial Hall at UK had been dedicated to the Commonwealth's World War I dead in 1929.)

The Coliseum bleachers prior to the renovation.

At war's end, ground was broken along Euclid Avenue (later the Avenue of Champions) directly in the shadow of McLean Stadium on Stoll Field for the memorial field house-auditorium. What arose from that ground was a work of art, a building in the modern style that was nevertheless timeless, with yellow bricks catching the sun like a gilded stronghold. Kentucky had seen nothing like it, and when it opened in 1950 the four-million-dollar arena—an almost unheard-of sum at the time for a building of any kind—was instantly a source of pride and near reverence for citizens of the Bluegrass. The versatile facility unified the state as a space to share both the grief for its lost youths and the preserved freedom to enjoy thrilling spectacles. For years, UK basketball games were opened with a prayer for world peace as an acknowledgement of the Coliseum's original dedication to personal sacrifice that had granted America a hopeful future.

The doors of the arena opened to the public on Memorial Day of 1950, when it was officially dedicated as a war memorial for the Commonwealth in a dramatic ceremony of oration, music, and prayer before a full house. Thousands of family members of the fallen servicemembers were in attendance. Later dedications were carried out at the facility's first musical performance and the inaugural UK basketball game. For the next three-quarters of a century, town and gown members of all types rubbed shoulders at diverse events in the indoor stadium. While Rupp's Wildcats kept on winning in their new lair, a bold public arts schedule also drew large crowds to see world-renowned figures at low ticket prices. Over the years, attentive crowds in Memorial Coliseum have witnessed U.S. presidents discoursing, famous musicians performing, community ceremonies being conducted, and top athletes competing. The men's basketball team moved their home court to Rupp Arena in 1976, but the women's hoops squad, volleyball, gymnastics, and other UK programs have filled the sporting void on the Coliseum floor. Big Blue fans have never stopped cheering inside Memorial.

As one of the state's most grand and consequential public facilities, surpassed in beauty and importance on its opening only by the capital building in Frankfort, the Coliseum helped to elevate Lexington's municipal aspirations. The city was now on the country's cultural map. Previously, the only public gathering halls in town had been the theatres on Main Street and the deteriorated Woodland Auditorium. While the state gained a beautiful and healing war memorial, Lexington received a facility suitable for attracting world-class talent, and its local basketball team finally had an arena worthy of its fame. Performing and competing in Memorial before sold out, appreciative crowds carried prestige. It was a sought-out venue, included on the tours of the biggest names in entertainment and a source of pride statewide. For many Kentuckians a trip to Memorial Coliseum, whether for a performance, a competition, or to pay respects to a lost warrior, was akin to a secular pilgrimage. When Rupp Arena opened in 1976 with twice the seating capacity and cutting-edge staging, more popular shows and events than ever came to Lexington, but less frequently so to the Coliseum. Despite the arena's continued use, its status as a top tier performance stage was soon a memory.

By 2023, Memorial Coliseum still stood regally on the Avenue of Champions but was increasingly showing its age. Scheduled for a major renovation beginning that summer, the structure was crumbling and peeling at the edges. In the recent years, massive scoreboards had been added to the south wall, the northern balcony had been blocked off, and the addition of the Joe Kraft Center had completely transformed the northern end of the building. Still, if one entered the front lobby, climbed a pedestrian ramp to the left or right, strolled along a curving concourse at the top, and selected a wooden folding seat above the playing floor, they would feel and see much of what their predecessors had in 1950. The building's rehabilitation has extended its useful life and raised amenities to current standards, including air conditioning for the first time, but it also has removed some of what has characterized the hall for three-quarters of a century. The original seating, concourse fixtures, internal color schemes, and other features, all as distinctive as fingerprints, are now lost, abruptly ending an experience shared by four generations. A timeless link for Kentuckians has evolved.

This volume remembers the first seventy-five of, hopefully, many additional years for Memorial Coliseum, and captures both its original and renovated forms. My wish is that it will strike a pleasing and nostalgic chord with today's readers while serving as a worthy time capsule for future fans of the Coliseum in the decades to come.

—Kevin Cook, August 2024

Note: There are several vintage videos online from different sources that record the original look of Memorial Coliseum and its surroundings during the 1950s. Interested readers can perform online searches with the following key words:

"Basketball by Rupp," a training video, circa 1950

"King Kelly Coleman Wayland," a video of the 1956 boys' Sweet Sixteen

"Wayland vs Bell County," more footage from the 1956 Sweet Sixteen

"University of Idaho vs University of Kentucky," a silent game film from 1955

"Adolph Rupp Individual Offense," a series of three short training videos, circa 1958

The Need For a Field House

In the Fall of 1946, the University of Kentucky found itself squeezed between two seemingly irreconcilable forces. The first was a tidal wave of World War II veterans enrolling at the school through the new financial support of the federal G.I. Bill. The second was the overwhelming popularity of its men's basketball program, shaped and perfected over sixteen seasons by Coach Adolph Rupp. While most of the additional students looked forward to cheering on the Wildcat athletic teams, the school's basketball arena lacked enough bleachers to accommodate every new scholar. Alumni Gymnasium, a brick neoclassical structure built in 1924, had seating for about 3,000 fans, far below the number of men and women expected to enroll by the time classes started on campus. There seemed to be no immediate answer for how to satisfy the rabid fan interests of the expanded student body, let alone the many basketball rooters already living in Lexington and throughout the surrounding Bluegrass region.

The financial assistance for college tuition and expenses provided by the G.I. Bill was broadening Americans' access to higher education – and straining the resources of universities across the country. UK, for example, simply did not have the dormitory capacity to accommodate all the male freshmen. Fall enrollment in 1946 would reach 6,600, well above the pre-war average of about 3,800, and this number would only

The Gymnasium wing of Barker Hall, UK men's first basketball home, 1903-1924.

Alumni Gymnasium, the UK men's baskeball home, 1924-1950.

grow in the immediate years ahead. As quickly as possible, the school began throwing up wooden barracks-like housing on available open ground, with hundreds of young men temporarily berthed in bunk beds on the open floor of Alumni Gymnasium until the new construction was completed. The spartan bunks must have reminded many of the freshmen of their recent military duty. Fortunately, the rough new dorms soon were ready, and Coach Rupp had his home court available for practice before the season's start.

By the time the 1946-47 basketball campaign rolled around in November, it was clear that the expanded campus enrollment would exacerbate the years-long problem of too many fans and too few seats in Alumni Gym. The facility's interior consisted of twenty-three ascending rows of bleachers on either side of the playing floor. In front of these on one sideline were the "box seats": three rows of folding chairs set up on low risers. Several hundred more spectators could fill in along the stairwells, endlines, windowsills, and various corners. Crowds perhaps as high as 5,000 had squeezed inside the gym during earlier years, but crackdowns by the local fire authorities during the 1930s had resulted in the limiting of standing room attendance.

The UK Athletic Association (a forerunner of UK Athletics), headed by Athletic Director Bernie Shively, realized that a difficult decision had to be made to effectively control game crowds. Prior to the start of the basketball season, the athletic department announced that seventeen home games would be played. Eleven of these would be set aside exclusively for the student body with the remaining six reserved solely for the public. Within a couple of weeks this plan was modified as the school recognized that given the sizeable student population, some were likely to be turned away as crowd capacity was reached. The solution chosen was to split the students into two groups, with each set allowed to attend six games depending on whether their individual ticket books (paid for through an enrollment fee and which granted entry to athletic events in the form of coupons) carried a serial number ending in an odd or even number. The general public was now left with five games designated for them (but with UK students excluded).

The Kentucky Wildcats were in the midst of the basketball golden era of the "Fabulous Five," a dominating collection of players. This legendary quintet helped UK win the National Invitation Tournament (NIT) in 1946, reach the NIT final the following season, then capture consecutive National Collegiate Athletic Association (NCAA) crowns in 1948 and 1949. The five gifted athletes, Alex Groza, Ralph Beard, Wallace "Wah Wah" Jones, Cliff Barker, and Kenny Rollins (who graduated in 1948) played an exciting brand of fastbreak basketball that seemed to produce unending victories. Demand for seats in Alumni Gymnasium was at its zenith.

The following year, campus enrollment increased to 7,500 and the number of home games was reduced to a slim eleven games as Rupp shifted his schedule to include more away contests at more lucrative venues. Additional students and fewer games in Alumni Gymnasium were not a recipe for satisfying the fans' desire to see their Wildcats in action. The UK Athletic Association decided to eliminate ticket access to the general public entirely, splitting ten games evenly between alternating student units (divided again by their odd- or even-numbered ticket books) and reserving access to one contest for University faculty and staff. This meant that the local community, remarkably, could no longer attend Kentucky games in Lexington.

Off-campus supporters wishing to cheer on their team still had some options. They could travel to Louisville for the two regional "home games" that UK played each year in the Jefferson County Armory, or seek to purchase a ticket illicitly from a Kentucky student. The latter was against University rules but a frequent occurrence. Patrons who looked too old to be undergraduates were a common sight in the gym stands. In fact, many of them had bought their tickets from a student. Of course, anyone with the financial means could also travel with the Wildcats to one of their far-flung games in larger arenas, where Rupp's squad played in front of immense crowds and earned substantial gates in places like New Orleans, Chicago, and New York's Madison Square Garden. There, Kentucky received the national attention and honors in which the supporters back home took great pride, even if they could only enjoy them from afar.

While students reluctantly began taking turns attending basketball games in Alumni Gymnasium during the 1946-47 season, the entire UK fanbase could look ahead with hope and optimism to the near future. Soon, ground would be broken just down the street on Euclid Avenue (now Avenue of Champions) for a new basketball arena, a massive field house-auditorium. The University assured students and the public that it would contain ample capacity for all who wanted to see the Wildcats in action. Never again, it was promised, would anyone be turned away at the ticket booth for lack of seats. But the reality would be far different and the era of restricted access to home games for Kentucky fans would only continue.

The quest for a larger arena to replace Alumni Gymnasium began in the mid-1930s when UK students, concerned faculty, and the school's athletic department began openly weighing ideas for a field house. This was to be a large all-purpose sporting facility where the football team and other sports squads could practice indoors during inclement weather, and where a basketball floor and bleachers could also be installed. Many articles appeared in the *Kentucky Kernel*, the student newspaper, presenting the various and shifting field house plans over the next few years. These proposals always lacked sufficient funding, which was in short supply during that era of the Great Depression, and the UK president, Frank McVey, was adamant that the University would not go into debt for a new athletic facility.

When Albert "Happy" Chandler became governor of Kentucky in December 1935, he immediately provided some political support for getting UK a field house. Chandler was a former athlete himself, having been a standout baseball player at Transylvania University in Lexington. (In later years, he would serve as the commissioner of Major League Baseball and facilitate the integration of the big leagues by Jackie Robinson in 1947.) While the governor could only offer $15,000 in state funds, he encouraged the school to apply for additional dollars from the Works Progress Administration (WPA), a Depression-era federal program that assisted with construction projects across the country. President McVey did indeed make ample use of WPA money, but he focused on much-need classroom and dormitory construction, placing new athletic facilities far down his priority list.

Nevertheless, between 1936 and 1941 ideas of varying practicality were put forward for a field house design. The first proposal was drawn up by students in the college of engineering and provided for a one-story building 100 feet wide and 180 feet long with a dirt floor. The pitched roof would be supposedly high enough to contain a punted football, and temporary basketball stands would hold around 4,500 spectators. It soon became clear, however, that even potential WPA funds would not be enough. In early 1937, Coach Rupp spoke to the Lexington Lions Club and threw out the idea of the city building its own municipal field house where his Wildcats could play home games in front of 10,000 supporters. It was a concept that went nowhere at the time but foreshadowed Lexington's downtown Rupp Arena four decades later.

In early 1939, Governor Chandler stepped in again to publicly endorse a field house for UK. Chandler had just witnessed overflowing crowds in Kentucky's Alumni Gymnasium for the boys' Sweet Sixteen high school state basketball tournament, and in his immediate excitement promised reporters that he would up the state's financial commitment to $50,000 for a new arena. The governor viewed the push for a larger sports venue as a political winner. James Graham, dean of UK's engineering school, caught the field house fever as well and talked of designing a forty-five-foot-high facility with 12,000 seats. He also envisioned incorporating 100 dormitory rooms beneath the stands to provide needed student housing. Within days, Graham was telling the student paper that the roof could be even higher, and four floors of offices and classrooms could encircle a central arena. A projected cost for this impressive building ranged from $200,000 to $250,000.

Of course, these numbers far outstripped what was available from existing sources as the Depression continued through the 1930s. Perhaps the most significant result of this latest field house proposal was its suggested site on Euclid Avenue across from University grounds, which would have placed it close to some of the few parking areas on campus. However, preliminary investigations by UK concluded that just the cost of purchasing the needed land along this street for the arena would be too expensive. For the first time, however, a specific site for a new basketball facility had been publicly identified.

In the spring of 1939, a novel idea was floated by city leaders and the University. What if, they asked, Lexington took on the funding and construction of a versatile municipal arena with chair-style seating and high-end acoustics? It could double as an auditorium and concert hall for all manner of events, making money for the city and serving as the homecourt of the Kentucky Wildcats. The estimated price tag for the building was the largest yet, and Lexington ultimately was no more able to construct a new arena than UK had been.

Throughout all of the brainstorming and creative discussions for a field house, UK President McVey was resolute that his school would not go into debt to build it.

He well-remembered the debacle of paying for Alumni Gymnasium fifteen years earlier in his administration. That building was originally to be funded by a partnership between the UK Athletic Association and the UK Alumni Association. However, both organizations soon experienced significant revenue shortages even as the projected arena costs more than doubled. The school's trustees were forced to step in, first to guarantee construction payments and eventually to fund most of those payments. In fact, the University would be saddled with debts from the building until the mid-1940s. McVey's made his position clear: "In all this discussion there is one point that I have insisted upon, and that is that the University cannot and must not go in debt for this building. I am sure that the Board of Trustees would welcome this construction if amounts could be found without increasing the indebtedness of the University." UK's president, then, would not stand in the way of a fully-financed arena but he would not be a prime mover for such an endeavor. As a result, UK's arena schemes continued to come to naught. Renewed momentum for an on-campus field house would have to wait for a change in UK's leadership, but that would not be long in coming.

When UK's hopes for a new basketball arena seemed to have been extinguished, the University inaugurated a new president, Herman L. Donovan, in the summer of 1941. Born in Maysville, Kentucky, Donovan was a UK alumnus and had been president of Eastern Kentucky Normal School (now Eastern Kentucky University) for thirteen years. He was committed to leading UK as a progressive flagship university for the Commonwealth, a vision that included excelling in athletics and building the long-proposed field house. Unlike his predecessor, Donovan believed that success in intercollegiate sports could spur increased attention and funding from the Kentucky legislature. He recognized a connection between the success of Wildcat football and basketball teams and the level of educational funding from the General Assembly in Frankfort. Winning programs would likely attract state dollars for a large capacity field house as well as other school needs, which would support more winning on the athletic field.

But Donovan envisioned a field house that would be more than just a sports facility. It would be a versatile building that would meet multiple needs of the University. Soon after taking office, Dr. Donovan gave an interview to *Kentucky Alumnus* magazine, outlining his plans for the school. He stated, "At present there is no auditorium on the campus large enough to hold the student body, no place where large agricultural meetings, sporting events, music contests, and other such gatherings can be adequately housed." What was needed, he explained, was a multipurpose structure that would accommodate indoor events of all kinds, not just basketball games. He was ready to submit to the state legislature a budget proposal for a "general utility building, which would not only provide for a gymnasium with a basketball floor where from 10,000 to 12,000 might witness a game, but also serve the University for an auditorium." It would be a combination field house-auditorium that would "be of enormous value to the University and to the entire state." Such a grandiose venue would be quite expensive, but President Donovan was betting that a multifaceted facility would be more acceptable to both politicians and taxpayers. The Great Depression was losing its hold on the nation as economic conditions slowly improved. Perhaps the future would be more kind to financing and constructing such an arena.

Within weeks, the unthinkable happened as the Japanese military attacked the American naval base at Pearl Harbor, Hawai'i. With the country suddenly at war, every available resource was directed towards the U.S. military. All large civilian and non-essential construction projects were put on hold, including any plans for a UK field house. Over the ensuing four years, nearly ten thousand of Kentucky's citizens would die for their country. Their sacrifice would one day be memorialized at the University of Kentucky.

While the University was unable to proceed with any campus building plans, Donovan and the UK Trustees moved ahead with whatever steps they could still take to be ready whenever the war concluded. When the state legislature approved $400,000 for the school to spend on general capital outlays, the University began buying up plots of land adjacent to Euclid Avenue in the African American neighborhood of Adamstown, which were mostly rental properties. By the middle of 1943, UK owned a two-block-square parcel of land on which to someday build its field house. In 1945, the University hired an architectural team headed by John T. Gillig to design a worthy building. During this latter stage of the war, UK's vision of the field house became grander, and the Board of Trustees resolved that the arena should be dedicated as a memorial to the state's war dead, a toll that had rapidly risen by the thousands. The decision to make the field house a Kentucky war monument raised its profile statewide, which over time attracted greater funding from the state government. UK also issued $800,000 in twenty-year bonds to help finance the project, which ultimately cost nearly four million dollars.

Excavation along Euclid Avenue began in the summer of 1947, and a swarm of workers undertook the steel framing of the building the next year. By the time the facility's form began to take shape in 1948, UK's President Donovan had long pondered how the building should be properly named. At the field house's cornerstone ceremony on February 22, 1949, he gave the key address and publicly announced his recommendation for naming the new building: "It is a worthy memorial to the 9,445 Kentuckians who sacrificed their lives for their country in World War II.... I shall recommend to the Board of Trustees at its next meeting that this building be officially named the Memorial Coliseum, and that it be dedicated to their memory." The Board soon readily gave its approval, and the noble purpose and symbolism of the arena were permanently established.

Here, then, is the history of this honored building in pictures.

What Came Before

Visionaries

An unidentified group of architects and engineers look over a scale model of the UK campus, circa 1940. The exhibit, used for planning the use of the University's land, reveals how compact the school was at the time and the future location of Memorial Coliseum. The layout is viewed towards the east, with Nicholasville Road running lengthwise in the foreground. The old football stadium (torn down in the 1970s) on Stoll Field can be seen immediately in front of the man sitting third from the left in the dark coat. Winslow Street (now Avenue of Champions) runs directly next to the stadium's left stands and towards Nicholasville Road in the lower left corner. Memorial Coliseum would later rise on the ground to the left of the stadium. Further down the right side of Winslow Street sits Alumni Gym, with the Student Union Building directly behind it to the right. The "empty" lots to the left of the football field were actually the contemporary location of the African American community of Adamstown until the mid-1940s. At that time, UK began to purchase the dozens of rented houses in order to build Memorial Coliseum. The modest wooden dwellings were completely razed, and the area remained empty except for spared trees until construction began on the arena in 1947.

The Coliseum's Future Home

An aerial view of the UK campus, circa early 1940s, looking to the south. The future site of Memorial Coliseum is in the lower left corner across from the football stadium. Euclid Avenue (now Avenue of Champions) runs just below the stadium. The historically African American neighborhood of Adamstown still remains for several square blocks in the bottom of the image, but will be demolished in 1944 in anticipation of Memorial Coliseum's construction. For several years, only the trees in Adamstown will be left standing. The concrete stands of McLean Stadium on Stoll Field (the extended athletic grounds that host football, baseball, and track events) are seen in their original size, but will be significantly enlarged in the late 1940s as capacity is expanded under new football coach Paul "Bear" Bryant. To the immediate right of the stadium is the spartan baseball diamond, and further down the road is Alumni Gymnasium.

Alumni Gymnasium

Completed in 1924, Alumni Gymnasium stands ready to host the Wildcats' home games on what is now Avenue of Champions, circa 1940. It was the first campus building designed specifically for basketball, replacing the two original makeshift courts that had been installed inside opposite wings of Barker Hall. On the upper floor of Alumni Gym were the basketball court, athletic offices, and the trainer's room, with locker rooms and more offices in the walkout lower floor. The school bookstore and post office were also located in the basement until a major flood in 1928 forced their relocation. The arena's construction was greatly delayed by poor weather and the bankruptcy of the general contractor. UK had hoped to play some varsity games there by February 1924, but its season concluded before the gym was fully outfitted. Instead, the Kentucky boys' high school basketball tournament provided the inaugural games in March of 1924, with the Wildcats finally taking the floor for the first time that December in a victory over Cincinnati. The architectural design of the building is Palladian, a classical style developed by the Italian Andreas Palladio in the 1500s during the European Renaissance, and which harmonized with UK's neighboring contemporary campus structures. The tall glass windows encircling the entire building are striking, although the bleachers inside the arena served to block much of the ambient sunlight from reaching the court. In recent years the building was gutted and completely remodeled in its interior as a fitness center for students as part of the Gatton Student Center. All of the front exterior windows were extended downward to full length, making the facility even more uniform and beautiful.

Not Enough Seats

A full crowd fills Alumni Gymnasium during the late 1940s. Players Walter Hirsch and Jim Line sit in their satin warmups and Chuck Taylor-model Converse shoes next to Adolph Rupp (left to right) on the Kentucky bench. Beside them are the tables of press row where scorekeepers, clock and scoreboard operators, and journalists sit. The tight facial expressions on the sideline seem to indicate an unusually tense moment for the Wildcats in their home lair, where they typically won easily. Coach Rupp, however, was a chronic worrier who often fretted during games no matter the score. To counter his anxiety, he sports his normal lucky game attire of a brown suit paired with brown socks and shoes. The many suits and hats worn by the spectators in the stands indicate the expected dress for sporting events at the time. Beside Rupp is the team's basketball locker, in which are piled extra balls and the discarded warmups of players presently in action on the court. Immediately to the right of Rupp sits George Hukle, the team's principal statistician. A career postal worker, Hukle kept detailed shooting statistics at UK practices and games, numbers that Rupp came to rely on heavily to instruct his players. Hukle eventually became the Wildcats' longtime equipment manager, a position that he would later turn over to Bill Keightley, a fellow mail carrier.

The packed crowd illustrates the contemporary need for a larger basketball arena. Enrollment had skyrocketed at UK (as it had for schools across the country) in the wake of World War II as young veterans took advantage of the new G.I. Bill. Coach Rupp began to schedule more and more games off campus to increase ticket revenue and national publicity for his team. Games were booked in Louisville, Chicago, New Orleans, and Madison Square Garden in New York City. In the 1949-50 season, the last in Alumni Gym, Kentucky played only ten times in Lexington out of a thirty-game schedule.

Adamstown

Top: A view from the top of McLean Stadium's north stands, across Euclid Avenue (later Avenue of Champions) to the community of Adamstown, circa 1944. The overgrown state of the houses (an individual on the sidewalk appears to be disassembling one of the structures for its lumber) likely means that the neighborhood is soon to be razed. It was in 1944 that UK settled on this quarter near the main campus as the future site of its large basketball arena, referred to as a field house at the time. Approximately seventy Adamstown houses were occupied by Black tenants and owned mostly by a small number of white landlords.

Bottom: Another view of Adamstown, circa 1944. This is the corner of Lexington Avenue and Euclid Avenue (now Avenue of Champions), looking east along Euclid. These are typical examples of the many small "shotgun-style" houses of the neighborhood, left to the elements before they are demolished. The grounds of the future Memorial Coliseum would reach this corner within a few years. Adamstown had originally extended several blocks westward, all the way to Nicholasville Road, at the turn of the twentieth century. UK had acquired land there on the north side of Winslow Street (which was eventually renamed Euclid) over the ensuing years to build a performance theatre, a fraternity house, and other structures. At the time of its final dismantling, Adamstown was reduced to the equivalent of two square blocks.

Constructing the Coliseum

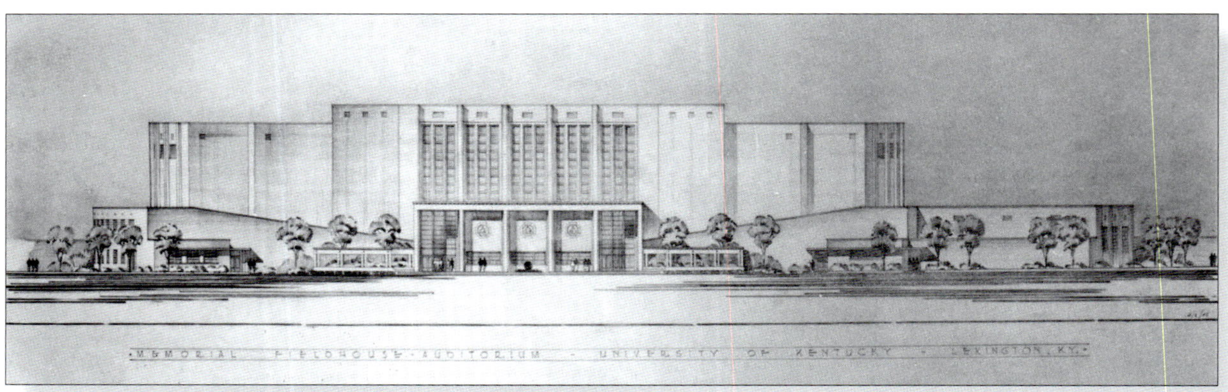

A Revelation

Top: The architectural teams' original rendering of UK's new arena in 1945, labeled as "Memorial Fieldhouse-Auditorium." John T. Gillig, an accomplished and veteran local architect, led the team, but the overall concept appears to be largely the idea of his associate architect Ernst V. Johnson, who had already designed a number of other campus buildings in a streamlined style. The building's curves, use of glass cubes above the main entrance doors, and strong vertical lines were elements of this contemporary modernist style, and represented a strong contrast to the University's older traditional structures of red bricks and classical columns.

Bottom: The final design for the field house, revealed shortly after the initial plan, differed slightly from the first effort through a slimmer overall width, windows stretching above the lobby doors, and zig-zagged brickwork surmounting the building's center. The varied and fancy use of external blocks is another indication of Ernst V. Johnson's structural and artistic influence. He was a trained mason and utilized that trade to work his way through college. The wings slanting upward from the central portico enclose the pedestrian ramps to carry patrons to the upper seating, an example of form following function in the arena's design. Johnson was known to include a dog somewhere in his renderings, and there appears to be a small canine at the building's right corner.

Ready for Groundbreaking

Above left: Euclid Avenue looking westward, circa 1946. The Adamstown dwellings previously on the right side of the street have been demolished but the neighborhood's ample trees still remain. The fieldhouse will be built in their place, while De Boor's cleaners, whose driveway is marked by the white picket fence, will remain directly next door. To the left is McLean Stadium on Stoll Field. UK would make use of the arena's pre-construction site by holding football pep rallies there.

Above right: A view along Euclid Avenue similar to the previous image, circa April 1947. The trees have now been cleared and the ground for the field house is undergoing its initial grading and digging for the pouring of the cement foundations. A groundbreaking ceremony had been held on April 1, with the UK band serenading a large crowd that saw Governor Simeon Willis and University president Herman Donovan turn dirt with a silver ceremonial spade. At the top left of the picture, Alumni Gymnasium is just in view. Across from it on the right side of the street is the long low building of Wildcat Bowling Lanes, with the Sigma Nu fraternity house behind it. At the upper right along Lexington Avenue are bungalow homes, which were still present as of 2024.

Finally Digging

An aerial view of excavation work on the field house in March 1948, looking north. The future site of the arena is in the upper middle of the photo, with McLean Stadium directly across Euclid Avenue (later Avenue of Champions) below it. Note the light towers above and outside the north and south stands of the football field. As the basketball arena was built, McLean would undergo its own expansion that would lengthen and raise both sets of permanent concrete seating. However, the light poles remained in place as the stands were enlarged around them, leaving the towers to rise in the middle of the future crowds. It would remain that way until the football team moved to Commonwealth Stadium in 1973. Expansive temporary bleachers, missing here during the football off-season, were added for games behind both end zones. Parallel to Euclid Avenue and directly above the excavation runs the residential street of College View. For years, the houses along this road sat within feet of the Coliseum, their yards backing onto the alley behind the arena. (A resident of College View would burglarize the Coliseum for over $11,000 in cash in 1957, worth over $100,000 today. See page 126.) To the left of the excavation along the northern side of Euclid are the Wildcat Bowling Lanes building and the Sigma Nu fraternity house. Across the avenue from these is the practice football field with its barely visible gridiron lines. The stadium and practice field together constituted most of Stoll Field, the sprawling athletic grounds that had occupied this area of the campus since the late 1800s. The concrete Depression-era wall, built by the federal Public Works Administration, can be seen wrapping around the periphery of the practice grounds, including along Euclid Avenue.

Cornerstone Dedication

The laying of the Coliseum's cornerstone took place under cold and wet skies on February 22, 1949, UK's annual Founders Day. Below, Adolph Rupp gathers mortar for the stone with a ceremonial trowel at the southwest corner of the building, where it can be seen today. Over his right shoulder stands UK president Herman Donovan holding a piece of paper, with Kentucky governor Earle C. Clements standing immediately to Donovan's right in a raincoat and hat. All would take a turn with the trowel as well as football coach Paul "Bear" Bryant and Athletic Director Bernie Shively. The trowel had been presented by a group of alumni to President Donovan at Christmas in 1941, to be used whenever the planned field house was built. The tool had lain idle for over seven years. The cornerstone carries the dates 1942-1950, signifying the project's total period from the beginning of land acquisition for the field house to the scheduled completion of construction the following year. The WKLX microphone leaning in from the right signifies that this was a major public news event carried live on radio. The young man in uniform is likely from the University's Army ROTC unit. The workman standing immediately behind the cornerstone at the far right carries his own trowel and level, ready to clean up the piled mortar and fix the block in place.

The Bones of a Great Arena

Above left: The fabrication of the fieldhouse's steel skeleton is well along in mid-November 1948. This view is taken from Lexington Avenue looking eastward, with the front of the building to the right. The tiered east and north stands can be seen inside, with the framework for the west concourse rising in the middle of the frame. The relatively lax labor standards compared to today is evidenced by the bold figure seen standing on a girder at the very top of the arena in the upper right, seemingly untethered to any safety device. Pre-World-War-II-model cars line the street because the nation's recent war footing between 1942 and 1945 did not allow for civilian automobile production during that period.

Above right: A view from the north "endzone" stands of the Coliseum looking south in February 1949. McLean Stadium, sitting across then-Euclid Avenue, is visible through the arena's unfinished lobby. The ceiling is forty-nine feet high, with twenty-five additional vertical feet of steel-lattice work for structural strength as well as space for ventilation and lighting. Massive stacks of yellow bricks sit on the floor of the construction site. The dirt floor will eventually be replaced by a layer of concrete, and the basketball court will be laid directly over that. This is the very bottom of the arena, with no lower levels. All offices, locker rooms and storage will be located behind the stands.

Slow but Imposing Progress

Above left: The reverse perspective of the previous picture, with the photographer standing at the top of the football stadium's north stands. The iron skeleton of the Coliseum is nearing completion, and its future skin of golden-hued bricks lies in huge stacks out front. Several temporary contractor's huts also sit beside Euclid Avenue (now Avenue of Champions), with a sign identifying Struck Construction Company as the general contractors. The other face of the sign reads "MEMORIAL AUDITORIUM FIELDHOUSE" (the name Memorial Coliseum had not yet been announced) and lists the names of the project's architects and engineers.

Above right: The concrete surface is ready to be poured over the steel frame of the Coliseum's west stands. At the top of the photo is the north "endzone" upper and lower seating, which will be fitted with bleachers. Through the lower openings in the north wall can be seen the back of the houses on College View right behind the arena. According to a newspaper interview in 1976, Adolph Rupp stated that the northern section of seats was added after he insisted that John T. Gillig, the lead architect, increase the original capacity from approximately 7,500 to 11,500. If true, then the building's initial layout only included permanent seating on the sidelines. According to Rupp, who gave no dates for his story, he asked Lexington mayor Mac Oldham to condemn Adams Street behind the Coliseum site to provide additional land for construction of a northern wing of stands. In reality, the street condemnation had already been planned for several years, but Rupp may have spurred the city into quicker action. Gillig verified Rupp's overall claim in his own newspaper interview in 1977.

Walls of Gold

Below left: Memorial Coliseum still lacks much of its exterior bricks as its construction continues in the spring of 1949. Parked cars crowd Euclid Avenue (not yet Avenue of Champions) in both directions, with a station wagon "woodie" passing between them. The photographer is peering over the top of the ten-foot-high concrete wall, topped by barbed wire, installed by the Public Works Administration (PWA) during the Great Depression as a security barrier around the athletic fields. On the left are parking spaces in front of Wildcat Bowling Lanes, a popular gathering place for students during this era.

Below right: The Coliseum is receiving its external cladding of yellow bricks, circa 1949. Scaffolding and tall, precarious-looking ladders support the work of the masons as they build the pale walls and outline the many windows. The swimming pool wing of the Coliseum is at far right.

Modern Facilities of a Sports Powerhouse

An aerial view in late 1949 of the UK campus and the nearly completed (at least externally) Memorial Coliseum at top right. Located across Euclid Avenue, McLean Stadium on the grounds of Stoll field has large, temporary bleachers set up behind both endzones, indicating that it is still football season. To the immediate left of the stadium, the UK baseball field is marked as a gridiron for football practice. Mounds of excavated soil from the Coliseum construction site can be seen piled along the edges of this practice area. Many longstanding University landmarks can be seen, such as Memorial Hall in the lower left. Likewise, some of the campus facilities are no more, like the tennis courts located close to Rose Street in the lower right.

Nearly Ready

The outside of Memorial is structurally complete in mid-1949 and the landscaping has begun. While the future lawn areas out front remain unsodden, the beds in front of the lobby entrance have been planted with shrubbery that will soon thicken. Cement walkways on the right lead to the building's side and back doors. Students will collect their basketball game tickets at windows on the right back corner (out of sight behind the swimming pool wing) and enter the arena through rear doors. In the upper right are the backs of houses along College View. A low chain link fence separates them from the Coliseum grounds. Because the football stadium sat directly across the front of the Coliseum, photographers had to position themselves to the side of Memorial to capture as much of the frontage as possible. This is why none of the ground level photographs of the building are from a head-on perspective until the mid-1970s. However, the Coliseum's design architect, Ernst Johnson, anticipated that one day the stadium would be leveled, and the full width of the arena's façade could then be enjoyed from opposite the main entrance. This occurred in 1974, when McLean Stadium was torn down after the UK football team moved to Commonwealth Stadium on the south end of the campus.

Memorial Coliseum as Monument

Names of Honor

President Herman Donovan had promised that the coming field house (later christened as Memorial Coliseum) would individually honor each Kentucky service member who had sacrificed their life for America during World War II. John Sherman Horine, a mechanical engineering professor, was chosen to fulfill this pledge through his skill in calligraphy. Horine had long inscribed diplomas and personalized slide rule cases for engineering students using his own special script. After World War One, he had hand-lettered on large sheets of heavy paper the names of over 2,800 Kentuckians who had died fighting for their country. These were displayed in Memorial Hall, the University auditorium dedicated to the state's fatalities in the Great War. Horine was given leave from his classes for the entire academic year of 1949-1950 as he painstakingly printed nearly 10,000 names, county by county, on outsized sheets. He made almost no mistakes, which would necessitate carefully scraping away the ink. The UK registrar, Ezra Gillis, had meticulously assembled a complete list of the Kentucky war casualties—no easy feat—as part of a nationally coordinated project. From this data, library assistants generated name lists which Professor Horine used as a reference.

Below left: Horine at his large work desk at one end of a library hallway where he labored several hours a day. A sliding straight edge was employed to pencil in guidelines for the names first, which kept the many columns of script perfectly straight. Among the thousands of names that Horine carefully drew with beautiful strokes was that of his own son, John Sherman Horine Jr.

Below right: Workmen carefully hang in a walkway recess the first of twenty-four large panels listing each Kentucky citizen killed in the Second World War. Looking on at the right is UK registrar Ezra Gillis. Each state compiled a comprehensive and accurate list of its war dead and missing for the U.S. War Department. Every one of Kentucky's 120 counties was represented on the long roll of citizens who served their country with their lives, beginning with Adair County. In the foreground are the frameworks of turnstiles to be unpacked and installed.

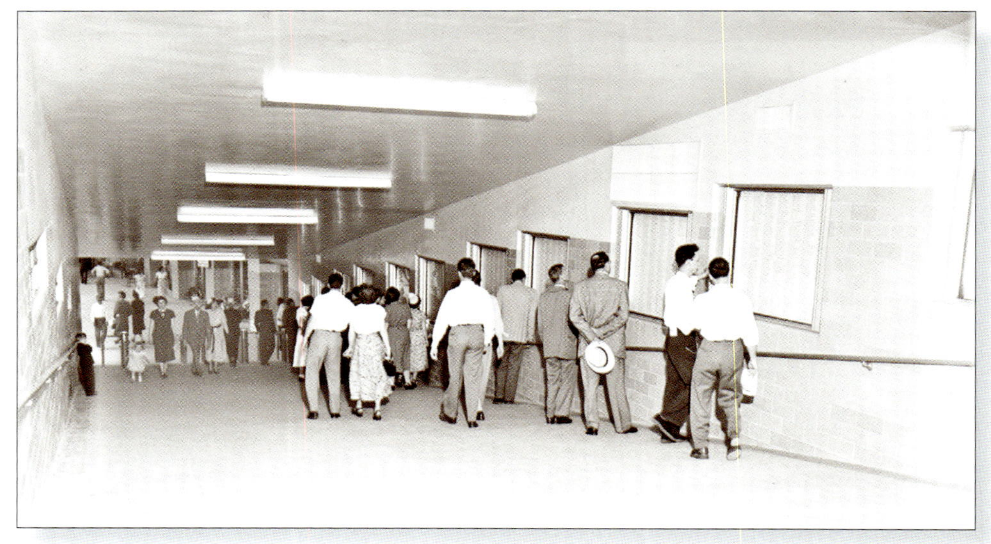

All is Ready

Above left: The Coliseum lobby prior to its dedication in 1950, with sets of external doors on the right. Five turnstiles wait at the base of the ramp to the eastern concourse. On the left, cigarette cans are positioned beside each of the doors that open onto the arena floor. These steel cylinders were once ubiquitous within public buildings. Above the central set of inner doors, a huge bronze tablet honoring Adolph Rupp would be installed in 1975. Just visible in the middle of the floor is a large "UK" in Art Deco lettering.

Above right: Attendees of the Coliseum's dedication on Memorial Day 1950 descend the eastern ramp towards the lobby, perusing the rolls of honor recessed in the wall. The inclined walkway without steps was designed to be accessible for the handicapped and elderly. The passage was steep enough, however, for the architects to include handrails along the walls. Also, the terrazzo surface soon proved too slick for some pedestrians, so non-skid adhesive strips were added to improve the footing. Eventually, carpet sections would be laid down over the sloped floor for better traction. The original turnstiles can be seen at the base of the ramp, where patrons' tickets were examined by attendants as they ascended to their seats.

Remembrance and Gratitude

A top row view of the combined Memorial Coliseum dedication and UK baccalaureate service on Memorial Day, 1950. This was the ceremony which consecrated the entire building as a war memorial to the state's World War II dead. Several rows of VIPs and UK academicians are on the large stage, with a forest of flag poles displaying U.S. and state standards. More banners were planted to the left and right proclaiming past graduating classes and the individual colleges. Before the dais sits the white-clothed University choir, with a student orchestra assembled in front of them. Graduating seniors and professors are seated on the floor and lower rows of the stands. There is nearly a full house consisting of the families and loved ones of both students and Kentuckians lost in the war. Every one of Kentucky's 120 counties was represented by a gold star family, with approximately 7,000 loved ones of the fallen attending. The Coliseum remembered its lost soldiers, sailors, and Marines by large, framed rolls of honor on the pedestrian ramps, brass stars mounted in the concourses, and the touching poem of loss and hope, "For the Fallen," chiseled in stone beside the main entrance (see page 34).

The service featured readings and music, including a musical arrangement of "For the Fallen" by UK professor of music Kenneth Wright. Dr. Daniel Poling was the featured speaker. He was the father of Army chaplain Clark Poling who, along with three other chaplains of different faiths, had given their lives to save other service members when their troop ship was torpedoed and sunk during the war. The chaplains' sacrifice had made them national heroes. At the conclusion of the ceremony, everyone in attendance was allowed to roam through the building's public spaces and examine the remarkable facility. For two more days, the University would keep the Coliseum doors open to the public, many of whom searched out names on the honor rolls. Throughout at least the 1950s, the arena's designation as a war memorial was remembered by short prayers for world peace before UK basketball games. These were offered by community faith leaders, and the prayers were immediately followed by the national anthem.

Not Forgotten

Below left: On the day of Memorial Coliseum's dedication, a young couple appears to search out names from Fayette County on one of the panels listing the thousands of Kentucky war dead of World War II. They were one of hundreds of families who looked for the names of loved ones on the rolls of honor displayed on the pedestrian ramps. The memories and effects of the long global conflict were still strong five years after its conclusion.

Below right: One of the carved stones flanking both sides of the main lobby entrance to Memorial Coliseum. This one is located to the right of the entry doors, reflecting the Coliseum's original dedication to Kentucky citizens who died in military service during the Second World War. As a military monument, the building has been subsequently rededicated to members of the Commonwealth killed in the Korean War, Vietnam War, and twenty-first century conflicts in the Middle East. The four lines at the bottom of the inscribed stone are taken from the poem "For the Fallen," penned by British poet Laurence Binyon. Written in 1914 near the beginning of the First World War, it was originally a tribute to British soldiers who had sacrificed their lives for their country. By the close of World War II, it was well known across the United States and frequently recited at military memorial ceremonies.

MEMORIAL COLISEUM

HERE IN STONE AND STEEL IS RAISED
A MEMORIAL TO
MORE THAN NINE THOUSAND SONS AND DAUGHTERS
OF THE
STATE OF KENTUCKY
WHO GAVE THEIR LIVES IN BATTLE
THAT WE MIGHT LIVE IN PEACE
ERECT AND STRONG AND FREE

WORLD WAR II 1941–45

"THEY SHALL GROW NOT OLD, AS WE THAT ARE LEFT GROW OLD:
AGE SHALL NOT WEARY THEM, NOR THE YEARS CONDEMN.
AT THE GOING DOWN OF THE SUN AND IN THE MORNING
WE WILL REMEMBER THEM."

Life Moves On

The crowd exits the Coliseum at the conclusion of the dedication ceremony and baccalaureate service on May 30, 1950. Near the front doors can be seen banners for some of UK's individual colleges, such as the schools of commerce and law. The white-brimmed hats worn by many men in the assembly likely reflect the contemporary fashion tradition of transitioning to light-colored headwear for the summer season beginning on Memorial Day. Note that the words "Memorial Coliseum" have not yet been chiseled into the stone blocks above the main entrance.

World War II Heroes

Right: The World War II rolls of honor were displayed in special recessed panels along the inner walls of both pedestrian ramps. A photo from 2023 of the first framed sheet shows the water damage along its bottom edge that has accumulated over the years.

Below left: A detail of the same panel's heading.

Korean War Remembered

Bottom right and left: Two photos depicting the first sheet of names for Kentuckians killed in the Korean War. These were hung directly on the wall at the top of the western pedestrian ramp.

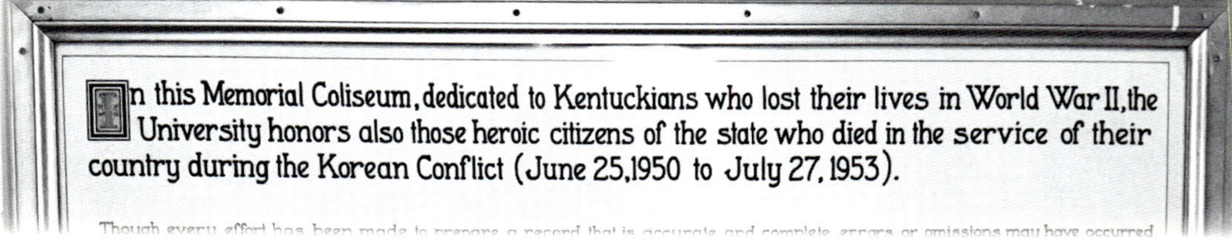

The Sacrifices Continue

The paired images illustrate the honor roll sheets of Kentucky's war dead for both the Vietnam War (top) and the later military conflicts (covering 1975-2006, bottom). The Vietnam framed panels were displayed near the bottom of the western pedestrian ramp, while the most recent fatality rolls were exhibited across the lobby at the base of the eastern ramp.

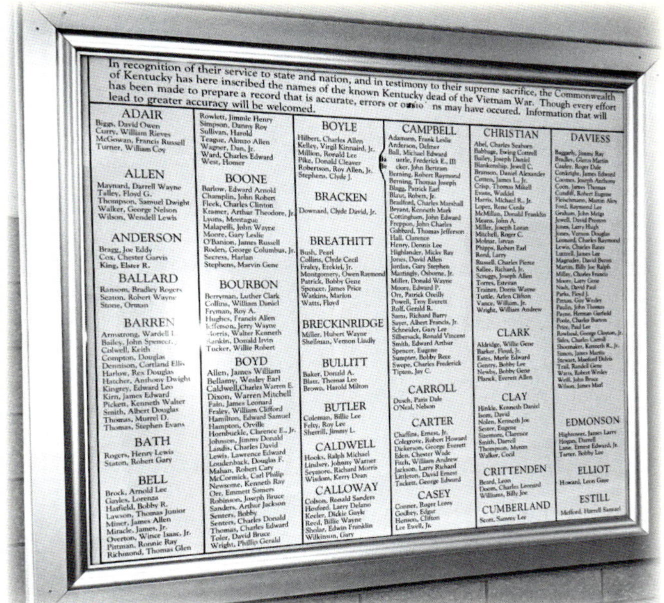

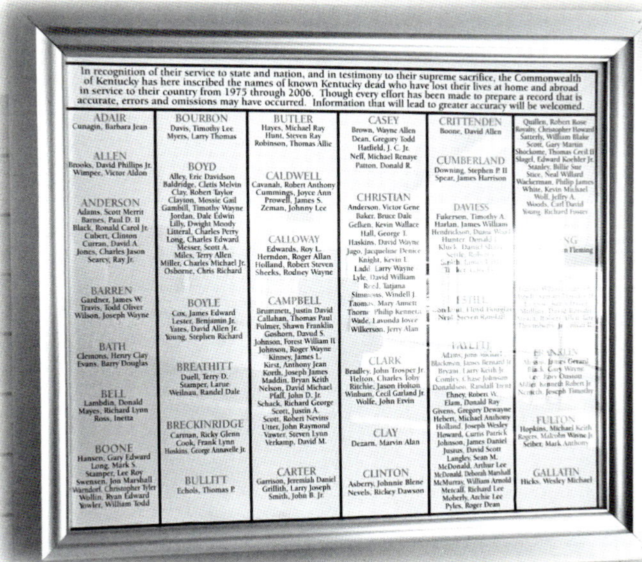

Memorial Coliseum as Sports Arena

Coach Rupp in His New Digs

Coach Adolph Rupp sits on the edge of his desk in his new Memorial Coliseum office in the Spring of 1950. He is surrounded by some of the trophies and awards accumulated in two decades as Kentucky's coach. The workspace was significantly larger than his previous cramped room at Alumni Gym, and he would soon fill the walls with framed photographs and mementos. His office sat at the center of the curving corridor running beneath the Coliseum's western stands, and adjoined those of the athletic director and head football coach. At Alumni Gym, the height of the door to Rupp's office had been a shade below six-foot-two, and he had used this fact to gauge whether potential guards were tall enough for his team. He was also known to loudly inform recruits visiting his Alumni room that they had just "entered the pearly gates of basketball" as they stepped into his domain. In the Coliseum, however, he had a standard-sized office door and it is not clear if he continued to use the same heavenly pronouncement.

The Crowds Came

An undated photo from the top of the west stands at an early game in the Coliseum, possibly the inaugural contest for the Wildcats against West Texas State College. Both teams have their benches positioned under the north basket on the left, with Kentucky in white uniforms to the far left. This is a change from the conventional arrangement in Alumni Gym, where teams sat along the sidelines. Helping to date the scene are the narrow six-foot-wide free throw lanes, which the NCAA broadened to twelve feet in 1955, and the two-digit scoreboard. UK added a third digit to the board for the 1953-54 season to track the high-scoring Wildcats' one hundred-point barrages. The north "end-zone" and balcony bleacher seating are visible on the left. The balcony would still exist as of 2023 prior to the Coliseum's renovation, but was not utilized. The seating directly below it was entirely removed for the addition of a two-story complex of training and meeting rooms in 1990.

In the foreground is the public side of the arena with fold-down, theater-style chairs for the well-dressed throng. On the walkway halfway down these stands are Boy Scouts in uniform leaning on the rail. Scouts served as the original Coliseum ushers for basketball games (as they had in Alumni Gymnasium) until replaced by the Committee of 101 (informally known as "Blue Coats") in 1967. Across the court are the student bleachers, not quite at capacity for this contest. The student band sits in the middle of this section, and it was their ritual to call out "Hello, Adolph!" each time the great coach emerged from the locker room before tip-off. A temporary tier of bleachers has been erected to the right of the court. This was usually the haven of the state legislators, each of whom was offered two complimentary season tickets annually. A tarp to protect the floor from the scuffs of street shoes and chair legs has been laid beneath the lower seats at courtside, and along the near sideline are the many reporters and radio broadcasters sitting at press row.

Opening Night

Below right: The program cover for the Sports Dedication game of Memorial Coliseum against Purdue University on Saturday, December 9, 1950. Coach Adolph Rupp had already scheduled a tune-up contest against West Texas State College (now West Texas A&M University) on December 1, perhaps to ensure a win to inaugurate the arena against an easier opponent. The Purdue game would be the third official dedication of Memorial, following previous ceremonies to recognize its status as a state war memorial and as a public concert auditorium. The Wildcats soundly defeated the West Texas State Buffaloes by thirty points, with forward Shelby Linville scoring the arena's first basket. (The first unofficial basket had been made by Rupp's young son, Herky, prior to the team's opening practice on the floor.) The game attracted an announced crowd of 10,000, not quite a sell-out. The formal sports arena dedication observance occurred at halftime of the Purdue game before a full house, also won by UK for their eighty-fifth consecutive home victory.

Below left: The court is set up for the official sports dedication ceremony of Memorial Coliseum at halftime of the game with Purdue. UK athletic director Bernie Shively is shown seated under the south basket after introducing UK Vice-President Leon Chamberlain as the featured speaker. Chamberlain stated that the new arena "reflects the vision and generosity of the people of Kentucky and their representatives in government, and it bespeaks the reverence in which they hold their honored dead...." Behind the basket are the temporary bleachers erected for each game. Multiple radio stations broadcast the Wildcat basketball games until the late-1960s, and the microphones at the podium carry the call signs of WHAS and WKLX. The congratulatory flower arrangement on the right is in the shape of a loving cup trophy. The flowers and stand would be moved to the end of the UK bench for the second half, almost on the edge of the playing floor. This was the facility's first capacity crowd. Although the public tickets typically were sold out each season, the students did not always claim their allotment of free spots in the east bleachers. These unclaimed seats could be purchased by walkup traffic at the ticket windows five minutes before tip-off.

The First Basket

Only one player could ever claim the honor of scoring the first competitive basket in Memorial Coliseum, and that distinction went to Shelby Linville of the Wildcats. Here, Linville controls the ball against Purdue in the second game ever held in Memorial on December 9, 1950. This was the night when the Coliseum was officially dedicated as an athletic arena, and the "trophy" made of flowers that was displayed during the halftime ceremony can be seen in the right background. The first basketball contest, however, had occurred a week earlier on December 1, when UK easily polished off West Texas State. Early in that matchup, Linville sank a short field goal from the side to open the scoring and make history. Linville was a six-foot-five starting forward whose best season was as a junior on the 1950-51 NCAA championship team, when he was selected to the All-SEC second team. After college he coached high school basketball in Kentucky and was eventually ordained as a Baptist minister.

Benches under the Basket

The UK Wildcats sit along the north endline and near the free throw lane during the 1950-51 season. On the opposite side of the basket sits the opposing team. The game would appear to be well in hand for the home team since the usual starters are all present on the bench, most wearing their flashy blue and white warmup suits with a satin finish. Sitting left to right in uniform are Frank Ramsey, Bill Spivey, Lou Tsioropoulos, Walt Hirsch, C.M. Newton (future UK athletic director), Bobby Watson, and Shelby Linville. Next in line are Adolph Rupp, Assistant Coach Harry Lancaster, and Rupp's young son, Herky. This was an impressive assembly of talent that season, with Spivey a first team All-American, Ramsey earning third team All-American honors, Linville recognized as an honorable mention All-American, and Watson being selected to the All-SEC first team. All are wearing black high top Converse sneakers. It would be several years before UK would switch to a white version of the same model shoe. Although the team benches had always been placed along one of the sidelines at Alumni Gymnasium, Kentucky sat underneath the north basket in the Coliseum from its opening until the late 1960s. During the 1950s, the visiting bench was relocated to the far endline, perhaps to better separate the competing athletes and coaches under game conditions that could make tempers rise.

Getting the Best of a Mentor

During the Coliseum's inaugural season of 1950-51, Adolph Rupp scheduled a blockbuster battle with his alma mater, Kansas University. The Jayhawks were led by the legendary Forrest Clare "Phog" Allen, for whom Rupp had played decades before but against whom he had never coached a game. Allen had already won two Helms Foundation national championships (essentially an unofficial title bestowed by a committee rather than earned through tournament competition) and would capture an NCAA crown in 1952. Rupp revered Phog, having played on both of his Helms championship teams, but still yearned to soundly beat his old coach and mentor before the Lexington fans. Kentucky's star seven-footer, Bill Spivey, would match up with Kansas' stellar center, six-foot-nine Clyde Lovellette. Both players were juniors who would earn consensus first team All-American honors that year. The game was played on December 16, 1950, before a standing-room sellout crowd of over 13,000. Kentucky delivered a shellacking while Spivey dominated Lovellette. The formerly undefeated and fourth-ranked Jayhawks were routed, 68-39, while Spivey scored twenty-two points, including dribbling for a full court dunk after a steal. Defensively, he held Lovellette to ten points, which was half the Kansan's average. Here, Spivey puts the defensive clamps on Lovellette, with Wildcat Frank Ramsey looking on. When the Jayhawk center fouled out with thirteen minutes left in the game, Rupp sat down Spivey as well so that no one could later claim that he had scored his points in Lovellette's absence. A quarter-century later, Kentucky would again face off against a Kansas squad early in the first season of another new home court: Rupp Arena.

Naming the Avenue of Champions

UK Alumnus Jere Beam climbs a stepladder to ceremonially re-christen a portion of Euclid Avenue as the Avenue of Champions in the spring of 1951. Beam had successfully proposed the name change to the Lexington Board of City Commissioners to honor the collective athletic accomplishments of the Kentucky basketball and football teams. It applied to the section of Euclid running between Limestone and Rose Street, passing by Alumni Gymnasium, Memorial Coliseum, and McLean Stadium on Stoll Field. Adolph Rupp's Wildcats had collected NCAA titles almost routinely in 1948, 1949, and 1951. Meanwhile, Paul "Bear" Bryant's footballers had achieved unprecedented success for UK by claiming a Southeastern Conference crown, playing in the Orange Bowl, and winning the Sugar Bowl, all between 1949 and 1951. Even the often- mediocre UK baseball team, which played on Stoll Field beside the football grounds at the time, finished with the SEC's best regular season record in 1950 at 11-2. Beam was granted the honor of "hanging" the sign. Also in the photo are (left to right) Athletic Director Bernie Shively, Coach Bryant, Lexington Mayor Tom Mooney, and Coach Rupp.

Coliseum and Stadium Face Off

This ground-level view looking east along the Avenue of Champions in the early 1950s makes it clear how physically close the Coliseum and McLean Stadium were to each other. The football stands, which had been raised higher in the late 1940s from their original construction, actually protruded over the sidewalk beneath. Photographers seeking to capture the full front of Memorial had to climb to the top of the stadium and look down through their camera lens. Street-level photos of the arena entrance were typically taken from a side perspective for many years, as in this image. It was not until the stadium was demolished in the 1970s that the Coliseum's entire magnificent frontage could be appreciated as the architects had intended.

Memorial Coliseum in Profile

A popular view of Memorial Coliseum looking eastward along the Avenue of Champions, from a postcard printed in the early 1950s. The side view, necessitated due to the proximity of McLean Stadium only yards away from the front entrance, reveals the slight concavity of the tall façade above the main lobby as well as the dramatic sweep of the arena's side walls. The modern architectural philosophy of "form follows function" is evident. The slanted sections extending from the front portico contain the rising pedestrian ramps, while the rounded flanks of the building enclose the curved concourses and seating that create a concert hall-like environment. The corner sign with "Avenue of Champions" indicates that the photo was taken after the street's name change occurred in 1951. Ivy has begun to grow on the Coliseum wall near its corner in the middle of the image. Over time, the vine would cover a large portion of this section before it was removed.

The Epicenter of UK Sports

Sparkling new Memorial Coliseum rises to the north of a packed football crowd at McLean Stadium, circa 1950. Seasonal steel bleachers fill both endzones, covering the backstretches of the running track that encircles the football field. In the bottom center, a private residence sits adjacent to the stadium grandstand like an island, surrounded by UK property and walls. Along Rose Street, which runs diagonally across the lower right, other homes have sold parking space in their yards for the Wildcats' fans, just as they do today near Kroger Field. The automobiles are so tightly packed around the houses that it is hard to conceive of how they could be safely reoccupied and moved. To the right of Memorial Coliseum is De Boor's laundry (with twin smokestacks), and to the arena's left across Lexington Avenue is the long building of Wildcat Bowling Lanes, with more crammed parking.

The Coliseum's Neighborhood

Another aerial view, circa early 1950s, of Memorial Coliseum and Stoll Field from a colorized postcard. To the left of the arena, in extreme proximity, is the De Boor Laundry with its smokestack, and four private homes next to it at the corner of the Avenue of Champions and Rose Street. Years before, De Boor had contested with UK over the acquisition of an adjacent property lot from Adamstown, with both claiming that they needed the land for future development. The Lexington city adjustment board ruled in De Boor's favor, providing them with some breathing room from the Coliseum grounds. The recent expansion of the football stadium can be approximated by the darker area of concrete visible in the middle of the far stands. The light towers, previously outside the stadium, are now within the seating area because the facility was enlarged around them. The reason for this is unclear. It may have been due to the lack of space beyond the stadium's periphery, especially along the Avenue of Champions, or to avoid a major relocation of material and wiring.

Basketball and Film Stars Meet

The UK basketball season of 1952-53 had been cancelled due to NCAA and SEC sanctions against the team for a point shaving scandal that had rocked the program. The cheating had occurred several years before, but the current Wildcats were paying the price. However, the boys' high school state tournament, already known as the Sweet Sixteen, was still held in Memorial Coliseum in March 1953. Kentucky stars Cliff Hagan and Frank Ramsey were on hand to watch the action. Between them in the above photo is Cleo Moore, a B-movie starlet visiting Lexington to promote her new film, which was then showing at the local Strand Theatre. The trio stands before the temporary bleachers assembled in the south end of the arena, a rather ramshackle construction of worn wooden boards. The stands contrast with the rest of the Coliseum's new and modern fixtures.

A Season of Exhibitions

The chronicles of Kentucky Wildcat basketball show no official results for the 1952-53 season. The sad reason is that there were no official games played that year as a result of NCAA and Southeastern Conference sanctions against the program. These were a result of a few Kentucky players' involvement in the widespread college basketball point shaving scandal of the late 1940s and early 1950s. Investigations by the NCAA and SEC found additional violations by Kentucky of impermissible benefits to athletes by local boosters. Both collegiate organizations prevented member schools from playing the Wildcats during the next season, leaving Kentucky with no competitors.

Adolph Rupp continued team practices throughout the year and staged four public intrasquad scrimmages in Memorial Coliseum to keep his team sharp and their rooters engaged for the future. UK fan lore often describes these practice games as having been played before sold-out audiences. In reality, the crowds were large but below the Coliseum's capacity. The first exhibition was held on December 13, 1952, with icy streets throughout Lexington. The modest turnout of 6,500 witnessed the varsity squad beat up the freshmen by thirty points. For the second practice game on January 19, varsity and freshmen players were blended onto teams captained by All-Americans Frank Ramsey and Cliff Hagan. A crowd of 8,500 saw the "Ramseys" win easily. A few weeks later, the same rosters faced off again and the "Hagans" prevailed. The above image depicts action from this contest, which proves that the exhibitions were intense affairs. Cliff Hagan (6, in blue) tussles with Hugh Coy (11) and Billy Evans (42) for the ball. (Evans would win an Olympic gold medal for the U.S. in basketball in 1956.) Jerry Bird (22) stands to the left. A final demonstration game occurred on February 28 before 9,000 fans. Hagan and Ramsey joined the freshmen in blue uniforms while the remainder of the varsity suited up in white and won by a nose, 49-47.

Grabbing Some Food and a Smoke

Below left: Although Memorial Coliseum was originally designed as a state-of-the-art multipurpose hall, when it opened in 1950 it did not have permanent concession stands in the concourses. Uniformed vendors carried baskets of snacks and drinks up and down the arena aisles during basketball matches, but customers walking the main hallways before and during games had to purchase their refreshments at congested temporary counters. This scene is from the 1953 Kentucky boys' state tournament, with concessioners in numbered robes serving up orders of bottled soda pop and other drinks in paper cups. Behind the workers are the concourse windows and a glass case displaying team photos of past Wildcat squads. As always during this era, cigarette smokers are well represented.

Below right: The crush of the crowd in one of the Memorial Coliseum concourses on the first day of the boys' Kentucky state high school basketball tournament, March 18, 1953. Although smoking was prohibited throughout the entire building, lighting up in the concourse was a common sight during an era when many adults enjoyed cigarettes, and tobacco was a lucrative crop for the state. There are at least six lit cigarettes and one pipe within the packed throng. The smell of tobacco smoke was long an integral part of experiencing games and concerts at Memorial.

A Sweet Sixteen

Opening day of the 1953 boys' state high school tournament brought a massive turnout to the Coliseum. Unlike the current tournament schedule, where half of the field plays the opening round on a Wednesday, the 1953 competition began with only two games being played on the first day. Here, Caverna High School from Horse Cave faces off with Louisville Flaget in the tourney's first game. The two-digit scoreboard shows a healthy lead for Caverna in the second half, and they would prevail 67-50. Somewhere on the floor is Flaget senior Paul Hornung, soon to move on to a legendary gridiron career as both a Heisman Trophy winner at Notre Dame and a Super Bowl star with the Green Bay Packers. In high school, Hornung was a multisport athlete who was selected second-team All-State in basketball and first-team in football. UK football coach Paul "Bear" Bryant desperately wanted Horning to play for the Wildcats, but the boy's mother was set on his attending the Catholic Notre Dame.

Adolph Rupp would insist on a new triple-digit Coliseum scoreboard the next year, with room to track Kentucky's expected high scoring. UK had reached 100 points in a game for the first time in 1951-52, and the arena board could only show double zeros. The Wildcats' lost season of 1952-53 (due to the point shaving scandal sanctions) delayed the installation of a new display, but in the 1953-54 season UK topped the century mark an impressive four times at home as stars Cliff Hagan, Frank Ramsey, and Lou Tsioropoulos poured in baskets.

Vendor to the Rescue

During the 1950s, refreshment vendors at the Coliseum wore wrap-around robes with an identification number on the breast, and carried peanuts, popcorn, and soft drink cups in wire baskets throughout the stands. Here, Lafayette High band members at the 1953 boys' Sweet Sixteen tournament reach for peanuts from vendor Billy Fryer, as band director Forrest Schenks lends a hand. In UK's previous basketball arena, Alumni Gymnasium, the crammed bleachers and limited walkways precluded the use of roaming vendors, so snacks and drinks were only available at counters in the lobbies.

The Birth of the UKIT

The Kentucky Wildcats, after practicing and playing intrasquad exhibitions for a year in athletic purgatory, returned to real competition in the Fall of 1953. That season Adolph Rupp and Athletic Director Bernie Shively inaugurated the annual University of Kentucky Invitational Tournament, a mid-December spectacle featuring UK and three quality opponents. Its purpose was to replace Kentucky's previously-regular treks to New York's Madison Square Garden and Chicago for high-profile games that put the team in the spotlight of the national press. However, the trips had also put the players in close contact with the temptations of big-city gamblers, leading to the point shaving disgrace. There could be no more sojourns to the large cities, so Rupp and Shively brought the competition to Lexington. Their idea was to invite three worthy teams to play a two-day, mini-tournament in Memorial Coliseum, the University of Kentucky Invitational Tournament (UKIT). Each program would share in an even split of a sizeable gate. All seats were available to the public because season tickets did not apply to the event and students were between semesters.

Opposite page: This image is from the inaugural UKIT final between Kentucky and the LaSalle Explorers on December 22, 1953, with UK prevailing, 73-60. (The night before, the Wildcats had defeated the Duke Blue Devils while LaSalle had bested the Bruins of UCLA, coached by John Wooden.) Cliff Hagan, number six, wrestles for a rebound with teammate Frank Ramsey. Lou Tsioropoulos' face is just visible to the left of Hagan's leg. At the far left is LaSalle's All-American Tom Gola (15), a junior who would lead the Explorers to the NCAA championship that season. (Kentucky would decline to enter the national tournament after a 25-0 season when Hagan, Ramsey, and Tsioropoulos were ruled ineligible to play as graduate students.) Lasalle wears unconventional sleeved uniforms, but they sport white Converse shoes in contrast with Kentucky's black models. The next season, UK would switch to white shoes and alter its game shorts slightly to a blue waistband with white belt. These would be the only noticeable changes to the Wildcats' uniform from the late 1940s until Rupp's retirement in 1972. The crowds at the first UKIT were near capacity, with people across Kentucky coming to town for Christmas shopping and the games. Coliseum fans were known to sing Christmas carols at halftime, led by Mignon Doran on an organ wheeled from storage beneath the north stands. (Mignon was highly accomplished on the piano and organ, the wife of Morehead State College – University after 1966 - President Adron Doran, and a fixture on the organ at the high school Sweet Sixteen for years.) All four teams received $10,000, a sum reportedly larger than that offered by other contemporary in-season tournaments, and which helped attract the stellar competition.

Above right: The 1953-54 Wildcat starters have been introduced and are likely listening with eyes closed to the pregame prayer for world peace. This invocation was given regularly during at least the 1950s, in recognition of the arena as a war monument. From left to right stand Lou Tsioropoulos, Gayle Rose, Billy Evans, Frank Ramsey, and Cliff Hagan.

Basketball's Best Meet in the Coliseum

The programs for the first two UKITs held in Memorial Coliseum in 1953 and 1954 are shown above. Adolph Rupp sought stiff competition from across the country to make the tournament a nationally-prestigious event. The first year, Kentucky came in ranked second in the nation, with Duke ranked thirteenth, UCLA seventeenth, and LaSalle at number twenty. The next season the assembled teams again were all nationally ranked. LaSalle returned, this time at number four in the AP poll. Kentucky held the top spot in the country, but their opening opponent in the tourney was Utah, sitting right behind at number two. Filling out the field was the University of Southern California with the lowest position in the poll, thirteenth.

Tasteful Victories

A celebratory cake has been brought out to the center of the Coliseum to publicly commemorate another sweet basketball milestone of the arena. The Wildcats had just nipped visiting Xavier, 77-71. Their homecourt winning streak, begun in Alumni Gymnasium, had reached an unbelievable 115 straight games and its eleventh anniversary since it began in 1942. While these were not round numbers, the cancellation of the previous year's Kentucky basketball schedule (as fallout from the national collegiate point shaving scandal) prevented the team from publicly recognizing the tenth anniversary of the winning streak's origin. The unbeaten home string would continue for another year, until the Wildcats had been victorious 129 times in a row on the Avenue of Champions. Until then, the pressure on the athletes in blue and white mounted, as each player desperately wanted to avoid being responsible for ending the incredible streak.

Pumping up the Coliseum Crowds

Kentucky cheerleader fashions of the 1950s are on display as female and male members of the spirit squad pose outside Memorial Coliseum in September 1954. The women wear an all-white ensemble of long skirts and sweaters, with bobby socks and saddle shoes, while their male counterpart sports dark slacks and sweater. At basketball games, the cheerleaders crouched on the wide bands of open space along the court's sidelines, waiting to spring up when the Wildcats scored and to incite the crowd with megaphones during timeouts. (Changing cheerleader uniform styles over time can be seen by close inspection of other photos in this volume.)

An Unlikely Loss

In 1955, five years after the Wildcats had moved into Memorial Coliseum, they had yet to lose a home game to anyone, a winning streak that had started twelve long seasons before in the old Alumni Gymnasium. The last home defeat to a Southeastern Conference foe had occurred three additional years before that, in 1939. The string of victories had reached a breathtaking 129 straight contests and seemed to have no end in sight. Logically, the run had to end sometime, but logic also seemed to dictate that a home loss would eventually come against a worthy opponent. Georgia Tech did not fit that bill when they visited Lexington on the evening of January 8, 1955, to face second-ranked Kentucky. The Yellow Jackets had struggled near the bottom of the conference in recent years and were in the middle of another losing season. Many UK students had yet to return to town for the spring semester, resulting in a Coliseum crowd of only 8,500, far from capacity. Kentucky played down to their Georgia Tech competition that night while the Jackets played over their heads. Still, with thirteen seconds to play, Kentucky had the ball and led, 58-57. UK's Billy Evans was dribbling up the court under defensive pressure when Tech's Joe Helms stole the ball near the Yellow Jackets' free throw circle. Helms drove towards his own basket and hit a short jumper to take the lead. There still remained eleven seconds of hope for Kentucky, and they managed to get off two shot attempts in that span. Neither found the net, and the shocked Coliseum assembly sat in near silence as the final horn sounded and Georgia Tech began to celebrate wildly. The *Kentucky Kernel*, the UK student newspaper, carried the sad news on its front page ***(right).*** The Wildcats couldn't wait for their return engagement with Tech three weeks later in Atlanta, where they were sure to get sweet revenge. Unbelievably, the Yellow Jackets prevailed again, 65-59, thus handing the Wildcats their only two defeats in SEC play that season. The stretch of 129 consecutive home wins still stands as an NCAA record, and no men's or women's team has come close.

Who Tipped It?

Dick Lenholt and an unidentified teammate scramble with Jerry Bird under the basket during Saturday night's calamity. Tech's Bill Cohen is between Phil Grawemeyer and Bob Burrow while Bill Evans and Bobby Kimmel anxiously await the result on the otherside.

Tech Stunner Halts Record 12 Year Victory Streak

By DAVE NAKDIMEN

In perhaps the most classic basketball embarrassment of all time, Kentucky's Wildcats lost a home-court contest to perennial SEC doormat Georgia Tech, 59-58. It was the Wildcats' first loss at home in 12 years.

Providing the chaser for Tech's poisonous brew was little Joe Helms, a pint-sized guard who probably committed one of basketball's all-time larcenies when victory, unimpressive though it might have been, seemed to be within Kentucky's grasp. For, with 13 seconds left in the game and Tech trailing 58-57, Helms pilfered the ball from UK's Billy Evans, pumped in a jump shot, and blasted over a decade of tradition out into Euclid Avenue.

For Kentucky, the loss ended a home court win streak of 129 games dating back to January 2, 1943. On that date Ohio State upended the Wildcats, 45-40. It was the first time an SEC club had whipped Kentucky on its home court since Tennessee turned the trick, 30-29, on January 21, 1939.

Also washed out was Kentucky's regular season win streak of 32 games. The last time anything wound up the evening ahead of Kentucky was on March 22, 1952, when St. John's knocked off the Ruppmen, 64-57, in the NCAA regionals at Raleigh, N. C.

Kentucky, obviously complacent and with an eye toward their Monday clash with DePaul, never seemed to take the Engineers seriously until it was too late. The Wildcats shot and rebounded poorly and showed little of the dash and spirit which marked their victories in the UKIT last month.

Although it was Helms' jumper which provided Tech's winning points, the lion's share of the credit probably was due their defense. The Engineers clogged up the area around the bucket, forcing the Wildcats to depend greatly on foul line deep one-handers and outside sets. Even when the Cats did get in for a layup attempt, they invariably missed it.

Although out-rebounded, 77-50, Georgia Tech gave a good account of itself under their offensive board. Tech had three men 6-5 or better and one of them, 6-6 Dick Lenholt, was quite a factor in the win with some excellent rebounding.

For Kentucky, no one seemed to play exceptionally well although Phil Grawemeyer collected 19 points for the Cats. Bob Burrow had a 16-point night, well below his output average since the opener. Linville Puckett played a fine floor game but he could not hit. He was not alone.

Both outfits encountered cold going in the shooting department. Tech could connect on only 18 of 68 shots for a 26.5 percentage. Kentucky was little better with 24 hits in 85 tries, a below-par 28.2 mark. The Engineers actually won the thing on the foul line with 23 free throws to Kentucky's meager 10.

Storming the Court

Kentucky senior guard Billy Evans is carried off the court on the shoulders of UK students after the Wildcats defeated Alabama on February 28, 1955, to clinch at least a tie for the Southeastern Conference crown. (No SEC tournament was held from 1953 to 1978.) Days later, Kentucky went on to prevail over Tennessee in the season finale to claim the conference title all to itself, before losing to Marquette in their opening round of the NCAA tournament. The photo here is proof that UK fans have "stormed" the court on various occasion during the program's illustrious history, although never at Rupp Arena. The UK online archives provide a link to the original radio call of the game by Claude Sullivan on WVLK, one of several "Voices of the Wildcats" that broadcast over the radio waves at the time. (WVLK was the originating station for the statewide Standard Oil Network. It was founded by Happy Chandler in Versailles in the late 1940s, and its call sign stood for Versailles Lexington Kentucky.) Billy Evans was the team captain in 1954-55, a season that also saw Kentucky's 129-game home winning streak broken in a significant upset by Georgia Tech.

A Ride Fit for a Baron

This may look like a scene from an auto showroom photoshoot, but it was taken on the evening of March 5, 1955, after the final home game of Adolph Rupp's twenty-fifth season leading Kentucky. To recognize his silver anniversary at UK, a group of alumni purchased this light blue Cadillac with whitewall tires for the Baron. It was somehow—and from somewhere—wheeled onto the court, to the visible delight of Rupp, his wife, Esther, and their son, Herky. Prior to the presentation of the car, Athletic Director Bernie Shively emceed a program where about sixty former basketball lettermen under Rupp were recognized. Many of these were at the game without Rupp's knowledge, and the entire celebration, he claimed, was a complete surprise to him.

The legend of Rupp's Cadillac has prevailed to the present day. A lasting and false narrative held by many sports fans is that football coach Paul Bryant left Kentucky for Texas A&M in 1954 because of an alleged slight. As Bryant himself joked for years, the UK alumni supposedly hosted a joint basketball-football banquet where they gave Rupp a Cadillac while Bryant only received a cigarette lighter. Bryant's anecdote (as thoroughly researched by Jon Scott on his website, bigbluehistory.net) was first used at a pre-Cotton Bowl football banquet in December 1951 and was clearly intended for a laugh. The following relevant facts prove this. First, Bryant had been coaching football at Kentucky for only a few months in 1946 when the Lexington Junior Chamber of Commerce held a dinner to celebrate Rupp's recent NIT championship. The Chamber presented Rupp with a promissory certificate for a new Oldsmobile sedan. Due to post-World War II production shortages, it was several more months before he received the actual car. Second, in late 1952, Coach Bryant was given his own Oldsmobile in thanks for his coaching record by a private group of program supporters, including the state governor. Finally, Rupp received his second automobile, the above-pictured Cadillac, a year after Bryant had departed Kentucky. Bryant had his reasons for leaving Lexington, but it wasn't because of a cigarette lighter.

Where Victories are First Won

Adolph Rupp rules over a disciplined practice in the Coliseum during the 1955-56 campaign. Rupp stands in the foreground in his customary khaki shirt and pants, with white sneakers. The far doors to the main lobby are all shaded to prevent outsiders from watching the drills. During his decades at UK, Rupp's practices were free of all extraneous noise and chatter from the players to maintain mental focus and ensure coaching instructions were clearly heard. Student managers were responsible for locking all doors and accesses to the court so that even late players would have to be allowed in by Rupp's express permission.

Mike Harreld, the senior student manager for the legendary Rupp's Runts team of 1965-66, provided the author with an outline of Coach Rupp's regular practice routine:

Harreld arrived at the Coliseum as close to two p.m. as possible given his class schedule. He first helped the equipment manager get towels and basketballs on the court, as well as a tub of ice water ready for the foot of any player that turned an ankle. Next, Harreld checked all the arena windows around the playing floor to make sure their blinds were pulled down for privacy, even the ones at the very top of the stands. Coach Rupp wasn't overly concerned with anyone near the roof spying on practice, but he didn't want his team looking into the sun when they were shooting a basketball.

Team members were expected to be on the court for practice by 2:45 p.m. (If they had a class near that time, then they arrived as soon as possible.) Practice began with the players individually shooting foul shots and warming up with medicine balls, pushups, and sit-ups. Formal practice began promptly at 3:15. Everybody had a basketball and for the next thirty minutes they diligently refined their personal repertoire of in-game moves, concentrating on making each and every shot. Harreld stated, "That went on every day all four years that I was there. It was a definitely established practice and the primary reason Coach Rupp's teams always shot well."

Harreld recalled, "At exactly 3:45 the players stop[ped] shooting and walked toward the center of the court to meet with Coach Rupp. It was suddenly as quiet as a mouse waiting for the coach to say something. Coach might have something to say about the last game or our next opponent, or if somebody had been featured in the newspaper he was going to get a bit of a chewing out, just to take any stardust out of his eyes. After that we went into drills and practicing our plays, and working on defense, concentrating on the other team's strength. And we usually practiced to at least 5 to 5:30."

A Young Legend

"King Kelly" Coleman was a basketball phenomenon from eastern Kentucky, who was far ahead of his time on the court. By the end of his senior year at Wayland High School in 1956, he had scored a national record of 4,337 points (since broken). He was considered one of the top players in the country as he averaged almost forty-seven points a game. That March, he led his Waveland Wasps to the boys' Sweet Sixteen state tournament in Memorial Coliseum, and the crowds packed in tight to see the high scoring wonder that most had only read about. He did not disappoint, but the Wasps were taken down by Carr Creek in a semi-final matchup. There was yet a consolation game to be played against Bell County, and Coleman closed out his scholastic career by setting a tournament record with sixty-eight points.

Below left: Coleman (number 66) grabs a defensive rebound against a Sweet Sixteen opponent as his teammates begin to turn downcourt in anticipation of a fast break.

Below right: Coleman battles for another rebound.

Home Cooking

The official program for the 1957 NCAA Midwest Regional tournament. In both 1957 and 1958, the Midwest Regional competition of the NCAA tournament was held in Memorial Coliseum. At the time, only sixteen teams played for the title, and the regional matches were the first two rounds of the national playoffs. The victors moved on to the NCAA championship semi-finals, known today as the Final Four. Kentucky qualified for the 1957 NCAA, beating Pittsburgh in round one in Lexington before being eliminated by Michigan State. The next year's Wildcat squad, remembered to history as the Fiddlin' Five, made the national tournament again. (Coach Rupp had called them fiddlers before the season started because he believed they weren't ready for their Carnegie Hall-quality schedule, which would require talented "violinists.") This time they won both regional games in the Coliseum, then traveled seventy-five miles down the road to Louisville's Freedom Hall, where they won twice more to become national champions. UK Athletic Director Bernie Shively was a longtime chairmen of the NCAA tournament committee, and his influence helped the Coliseum and Louisville's Freedom Hall to serve frequently as game sites in the 1950s and 1960s. Although common at the time, NCAA tournament teams are no longer allowed to play games in their home arenas.

The Tough and Talented Jerry West

Kentucky's John Crigler (32) guards West Virginia's Jerry West in the 1957 University of Kentucky Invitational Tournament. Also on the court for Kentucky from left are Ed Beck (34), Vernon Hatton (52), and Johnny Cox. West led the Mountaineers through three consecutive UKITs, winning the competition twice. Each of these annual classics featured a memorable battle with the host school. In December 1957, the Mountaineers beat the Wildcats' Fiddlin' Five, 77-70. The next year West was unstoppable, pouring in thirty-six points with a broken nose as Rupp declared that he was the best player he had ever seen. However, it was not enough as UK won, 97-91. The rubber match occurred in December 1959, and West Virginia triumphed again, 97-90, with West tossing in thirty-three points while suffering another busted nose from an elbow in the first half. The UKIT remained a prestigious event for the men's program while the Coliseum was its home, but the level of competition slipped as additional holiday season tournaments across the country competed for quality entrants. After 1962, the UKIT hosted no nationally-ranked visitors until Princeton played in 1971.

Some Changes Inside the Coliseum

A full view of the Kentucky court during the 1957-58 season, the year of UK's NCAA champion Fiddlin' Five. The southern bleachers, at the top of the picture, are surprisingly empty. The Wildcats' bench remains under the near basket where it had been since the Coliseum opened. The UK warmup jackets display a large Wildcat head, as they had since the 1940s. The opponents' bench, which was originally at the same end of the floor as Kentucky's, is now at the opposite baseline. Along the right sideline are the cheerleaders in front of the tables of press row. Stretching from beneath the bottom seating on both sides of the court are grey tarps that protected the court's surface from scuffs and scratches. The free throw lanes are twice as broad as they had been two seasons before. The lanes were widened by the NCAA as it followed the NBA, which had made the same change in 1951 in response to the offensive dominance of big men like George Mikan. The tall centers now had to move further from the basket to avoid three-second violations.

A Shot for the Ages

It was December 7, 1957, the year of Kentucky's Fiddlin' Five. The formidable Temple Owls and their All-American Johnny Rogers visited the Coliseum for a clash of top teams early in the season. The battle on the court was closely contested from the opening tip, and regulation ended with the score knotted at sixty-five. Senior UK guard Vernon Hatton's late free throws had tied the game and sent it into overtime. Late In the extra period, Rogers hit a jumper to put Temple up by two with just three seconds left. When Kentucky's Adrian Smith launched a half-court heave that missed at the buzzer, many Wildcat fans headed for the exits. However, Kentucky regained life when the referees ruled that they had managed to call time-out with one second still left. Claude Sullivan was calling the game for radio station WVLK and gently chided the departing crowd for its lack of faith: "This could be the most thrilling play of the season, you know." John Crigler inbounded the ball to Hatton, who heaved the ball from halfcourt and over a lunging Johnny Rogers. (The image above captures the instant before the shot is taken, as Crigler runs by to the right.) The forty-seven-footer sliced through the net and tied the game again. The explosion of sound from the loyal fans brought the deserters running back from the concourses, as they paid the price for their lack of faith. The tense struggle continued through two additional overtimes until Kentucky prevailed, 85-83. The action had been so nerve-racking that former Lexington city commissioner William Baughn suffered a fatal heart attack in the stands while he watched the final anxious seconds of regulation.

A nail was later pounded into the spot from where Hatton had made his miracle shot, which continued a tradition that had started in Alumni Gym of marking lengthy field goals. In later years, a painted star was added around Hatton's nail, and that section of the floor was presented to him when the Coliseum court was replaced for the first time in 2007.

Rupp Fired Up

Coach Adolph Rupp leaps from the bench to bellow either instructions or displeasure while his longtime assistant coach, Harry Lancaster, sits placidly next to him. Members of the 1958 NCAA championship team, christened by Rupp as the Fiddlin' Five, watch the action from the bench. From left, these are Ed Beck, Vernon Hatton, Adrian Smith, and John Crigler. The team was not as strong as Rupp's previous national championship squads, losing six times. However, their quality of play peaked late in the year and they won the NCAA title by beating the Seattle University and their star, Elgin Baylor.

Coach Rupp would keep the location of his home bench under the north basket until the late 1960s, but the reasons for this are unclear. It was suggested to the author by the late Coach Joe B. Hall that having the benches underneath the baskets may have been an effort to preserve unobstructed views of the court from the premium box seats on the sideline. However, press row tables set up in place of the benches likely blocked the same sightlines. Baseline seating may have benefitted Rupp by allowing him to yell instructions and encouragement when his team was shooting at the near basket (presumably in the second half). Prior to the 1961-62 season, coaches were given a technical foul when they verbally directed their squads outside of timeouts and halftime. The Baron may have found it easier to get around this prohibition when he was physically close to the action under the goal.

Wildcats with Swagger

The UK bench and Coliseum sideline, circa 1960. The Kentucky bench is still along the north baseline, with a congested press row to the right. The several banners hanging from the courtside tables announce the various radio stations and networks that broadcast the Wildcat action to every corner of the state and beyond. The UK reserves wear their glossy warmup tops, with the backs boasting in white script:

Kentucky
N.C.A.A. Champs
'48-'49-'51-'58

Two Courts in One

This intriguing picture from the 1959 UK yearbook shows the Coliseum floor configured for high school dimensions, probably during that year's boys' Sweet Sixteen state tournament. The scholastic game is played on a court ten feet shorter than for colleges, and in this case the high school endlines and repositioned free throw lines have been added directly onto the more expansive collegiate surface. Players and fans likely felt as if they were seeing double, and referees had to pay close attention to the correct floor markings. The excitement of the boys' state championship competition matched that of the UK Wildcats' games. The large crowd and media presence seen here were common, with press tables lining two sides of the playing floor and radio banners visible courtside. When Memorial Coliseum opened in 1950, the boys' and girls' state tournaments moved from the Louisville Armory to Lexington because of the greater crowd capacity. After Louisville's Freedom Hall opened with even more seating in 1956, the two cities alternated hosting the tournament until it moved permanently to Louisville in 1965. Not until after Rupp Arena opened did the event return to Lexington in 1981.

Battle with the Buckeyes

Kentucky closed out the 1950s in the Coliseum with a memorable matchup against Ohio State. The Wildcats, ranked thirteenth nationally, and the third-ranked Buckeyes squared off in Memorial on December 28, 1959. Kentucky fell behind by fifteen points early in the game, and by halftime Ohio State already had scored 59 points. In the locker room, Coach Rupp lamented to his assistant, Harry Lancaster, that his boys were going to give up 100 points for the first time ever. UK made a stalwart comeback to win, 96-93, but it was the Buckeyes who went on to capture the NCAA title later that season. Above, Ned Jennings puts up a hook shot for Kentucky over Jerry Lucas. Ohio State's John Havlicek is to the immediate left of Lucas. Both Havlicek and Lucas were college All-Americans and NBA All-Stars, as well as members of the Naismith Memorial Basketball Hall of Fame. A third member of the Hall of Fame stayed on the Buckeyes' bench that day: future coach of Indiana University Bobby Knight. Along the far sideline are the crouched Kentucky cheerleaders, well in front of the first row of spectators. The Coliseum was renowned for the loudness of its crowds, despite the relatively large distance between the fans and the playing floor. This spacing resulted from the curved seating plan alongside the court, which angled seats towards the center of the arena for concert hall-style viewing.

Practice Discipline

Below left: A khaki-clad Adolph Rupp conducts a quiet practice in the Coliseum, circa 1960. His squad wears the common practice togs of the era – white tank tops and dark blue shorts. Concourse lights break through the dark wall of the two-tiered stands. At the very top of the seating, just beneath the ceiling, can be seen shaded exterior windows, outlined by daylight at their edges. Rupp directed team managers to pull the shades of the upper windows to prevent the sun from blinding his shooters, while the glass lobby doors at court level were to be covered to conceal practice sessions from opponents' eyes. A dreaded command from a coach to a player was to "get a wall!" as punishment for some mental blunder. The offender was required to run up the stairways to the very top wall above the last row of seats, then safely but expeditiously make their way back down. According to Cliff Hagan, this discipline may have originated in 1951 with Dale Barnstable, a former Wildcat and then-high school coach helping the team prepare for a post-season international tournament in Puerto Rico. The wall run was a regular part of Joe B. Hall's training sessions once he became head coach in 1972. Some players were reportedly skilled at giving the appearance of running to the top while only going halfway.

Exhibition Basketball Game

BOSTON CELTICS vs. ST. LOUIS HAWKS

Honoring UK's

FRANK RAMSEY — CLIFF HAGAN

Tuesday, October 17 — 8:00 P.M. (EST)

Memorial Coliseum—Lexington, Kentucky

Tickets: $2.60 and $1.55 – All Seats Reserved

Mail Orders to: UK Alumni Association, University of Kentucky, Lexington, Kentucky

Checks Payable to: UK Alumni Association

Benefit of Endowment and Scholarship Funds

General Ticket Sale Starts Sept. 1 at Graves-Cox Co.

(Over-counter sales only—no mail orders)

A Civil Rights Travesty

Opposite page, right: What was envisioned as a happy reunion between Kentucky fans and former Wildcat stars in October 1961 became instead a nationally embarrassing episode for the city of Lexington. The UK Alumni Association reserved Memorial Coliseum for a fundraising event that would endow the Association and finance student scholarships. The attraction was a preseason professional basketball exhibition between the NBA's top teams, the Boston Celtics and St. Louis Hawks. The scrimmage was particularly attractive to Kentucky fans because Boston featured former Wildcat All-American Frank Ramsey, while the St. Louis squad included his former teammate and fellow All-American Cliff Hagan. An advertisement for the event in the UK alumni magazine, *Kentucky Alumnus*, appears here. However, there was a potential problem in accommodating the NBA teams' Black players, including league MVP Bill Russell of the Celtics.

In the early 1960s, many Lexington businesses still refused service to African Americans, or relegated them to areas separate from white patrons. In Kentucky and other Southern states, businesses had the right to deny service to anyone for almost any reason, including race. The NBA teams were to spend a night in Lexington's downtown Phoenix Hotel, where African Americans were not normally welcome. Representatives from the Alumni Association and Hawks personally met with hotel management to ensure that all the professional athletes would be able to stay at the Phoenix and eat in its restaurant. Everything seemed to be in order when the players checked into their rooms early on the day of the game. Then Sam Jones and Tom Sanders, Black members of the Celtics, sat down for a meal in the hotel's coffee shop rather than the restaurant. There, apparently, the staff had not been informed of the agreement and refused to serve them. Sanders and Jones immediately left the shop and related the incident to their Black teammates, Bill Russell, K.C. Jones, and Al Butler. The five found their coach, Red Auerbach, and let him know that they were boycotting the game and flying home that very night. Every African American player on both teams, seven in all (including Cleo Hill and Woody Sauldsberry of the Hawks), joined the protest and left Lexington. Auerbach understood their decision, but with only a few hours left before the evening exhibition he felt that the game should go on. Many tickets had been sold and, he believed, it was for a good cause. Ramsey and Hagan also supported their Black teammates, but decided to play for the same reasons as Auerbach's and because they were to be specially honored at halftime.

Bottom right: The exhibition did indeed go on with only white athletes on the court, and the approximately 9,000 in attendance were never informed why their teammates were not present. After the game the remaining Celtics and Hawks signed autographs for young fans, both Black and white. The Lexington chapter of the Congress for Racial Equality (CORE), a civil rights organization, had already been demonstrating against local businesses with discriminatory practices, and soon its picket lines spread to the Phoenix Hotel. One such protest outside the Phoenix's coffee shop in December 1961 is seen in the photo.

Stall Ball

Although Kentucky usually played basketball at a frenetic pace under Adolph Rupp, Mississippi State won for the first time ever in Lexington in February 1962 by holding the ball for long stretches. This was an era when State was a league power, winning three outright SEC titles and sharing another with UK between 1959 and 1963. Here, the Bulldogs (their nickname had officially changed from Maroons only the year before) are already in a stall formation less than two minutes into the game. The bored Wildcats stand with hands on hips, including Cotton Nash (44) and Roy Roberts (23). In response, the Kentucky fans tossed paper cups onto the floor in anger. Interestingly, Kentucky appears to be playing a form of zone defense against the stall tactic. Rupp, who always preferred a man-to-man defense, did not intentionally install his first zone defense, a 1-3-1, until the next season. Even then, he refused to refer to it as a zone, insisting to the press with a straight face that it was actually a "stratified, transitional, hyperbolic paraboloid." Next to the player holding the basketball are banners for WBLG and Kentucky Central Insurance Companies radio networks, two of several radio systems broadcasting Wildcat games at the time. Claude Sullivan and Cawood Ledford, the two most popular announcers, called the season's games for the Standard Oil Network and WHAS, respectively. The large size of the crowd is evidenced by the number of fans standing in the concourse along the top of the photo. Ninth-ranked State won this game over number-two Kentucky, 49-44, and celebrated by placing a memorial wreath atop the home basket (the same wreath that Kentucky had left in Starkville after prevailing over Mississippi on the road the year before) and cutting down the net as a trophy.

Focus in the Huddle

It's a time-out during the 1962-63 season, and Adolph Rupp looks straight into the eyes of senior guard Scotty Baesler, his floor general, to give instructions. The Wildcats finished the year with a disappointing 16-9 record, but the competitive fire never left the coach nor his players. After graduation, Baesler became a lawyer and then a longtime Kentucky politician. He was mayor of Lexington from 1982 to 1993, followed by three terms in the U.S. House of Representatives.

All Eyes

Not every capacity crowd went home happy from Memorial Coliseum. One such time was the night of January 5, 1963. Kentucky and Georgia Tech grappled through regulation and overtime but remained deadlocked. With a handful of seconds remaining in a second overtime, the Yellow Jackets led by a point. Kentucky's Roy Roberts is shown rising for a potentially winning shot from the corner, his teammates only an arm's length away on the bench and every eye in the house upon him. The attempt rolled off the rim and Tech escaped with the win. Coach Rupp can be partially seen in his dark coat and tie beneath the left arm of Georgia Tech's number 32.

High Cotton

Below left: Cotton Nash, a three-time All-American at UK in the early 1960s, is perhaps somewhat overlooked in the pantheon of Wildcat greats. He had the misfortune of playing on very good teams that never advanced to the NCAA finals, which would have elevated his legacy. In his first varsity game, he treated the Coliseum fans to a seventeen-rebound, twenty-five-point performance, one of the greatest debuts ever by a Wildcat. When he graduated in 1964, he stood at the top of Kentucky's scoring list with 1,770 points over three varsity seasons. This mark was later passed by Dan Issel in 1970, the current career points leader with 2,138. (Nash is now ninth on the UK career list.) Nash is seen here wiping his hands dry on the padding of the goal stanchion, a habit he followed to prepare himself for accurate shooting.

Below right: Nash receives foot therapy from trainer Joe Brown as Coach Adolph Rupp looks on. The trainer's room for the men's basketball team was near their locker room underneath the Coliseum stands. The walls are built with the distinctive large yellow bricks found throughout the Coliseum. Visible between Rupp and Brown is an adjacent room with bunk beds, which served an important game-day purpose for Kentucky. For night contests at home, Coach Rupp and Coach Joe B. Hall directed their players to take a pregame nap after the team meal, either in their dorm room or in the Coliseum beds. While they rested, the Wildcats were expected to mentally prepare for the evening's athletic challenge.

Bright Lights

During the 1960s, a spotlight from above the Coliseum's north balcony was shone on Kentucky's starting five as they were introduced in front of their endline bench. The light was also used to illuminate the graduating upperclassmen on Senior Day. Here, the starters for the 1963-64 Wildcats enjoy their moment in the artificial sun, including (left to right) Randy Embry (11), Terry Mobley (25), and Cotton Nash (44). The other starters are not clearly identifiable but are likely Larry Conley and Ted Deeken.

Pregame Buzz

The excitement of a UK basketball game at the Coliseum often began well before tip-off. In this photo from the 1963-64 season, students in the foreground crowd the east sideline in front of their seating sections as the Wildcats take their pregame warmups. Across the way, the denizens of press row as well as season ticket holders also can't seem to sit still due to the energy in the arena.

Chaos on the Court

Home losses by the Wildcats in the Coliseum were rarities, and this victory over Tennessee in January 1964 was already well-decided when the final horn sounded. However, Kentucky had committed a late foul and Danny Schultz of the Volunteers was permitted two free throws with no time left on the clock. This led to the bizarre scene that was permitted at the time. Instead of the referees clearing the area, police officers, cheerleaders, and various teammates were allowed to crowd all around. Despite these distractions, Schultz sank both charity tosses and Tennessee went home with "only" a nine-point loss.

Sit-Down for 700

Coach Rupp's squads were so consistently successful over so many years that there always seemed to be another career milestone to be celebrated. On February 8, 1964, Kentucky overwhelmed Mississippi for Rupp's seven hundredth win. The post-game observance had a casual look, as the coach, team, and associates gathered at one end of the floor in an oval of chairs. Players from past teams spoke in tribute to the Baron as the crowd looked on from their seats.

The Man in the Brown Workwear

Adolph Rupp kneels above the distinctive center jump circle "K" in the Coliseum, circa the mid-1960s. He fingers an "Adolph Rupp" signature basketball, used at Wildcat home games. Over several decades, various manufacturers produced a Rupp-model ball. For many of his coaching years at Kentucky, Adolph Rupp and his assistants wore starched khaki outfits of long-sleeved shirts and slacks. Except for his rubber-soled Converse tennis shoes, Rupp looked the part of an army sergeant, in keeping with the strict manner in which he ran practices. No extraneous talk was allowed from the players, few outside observers were allowed to watch (exterior doors were locked and windows curtained off), and the varied drills were timed to the second. Witnesses claim that the Baron began to wear the brown workman's clothing after he visited Europe in the aftermath of the Second World War, helping to set up recreational programs for the Armed Forces. It was there, supposedly, that he was introduced to the tan work uniforms in the army post exchanges and purchased several sets. The image of military-like precision, efficiency, and discipline likely fit the principles he desired for his basketball program. However, Rupp can be spotted wearing khakis as early as 1941 in the annual UK yearbook. The tan uniforms may also have served as a counterpart to Rupp's lucky game attire: all-brown suits with matching ties, shoes, and socks. He was popularly known nationwide as "The Man in the Brown Suit." The practice khakis did not survive the transition to Joe B. Hall as head coach in 1972. Hall clothed his staff in modern UK-branded golf shirts and polyester coaching pants and shorts.

What a Ride for the Runts

Above left: Perhaps Adolph Rupp's most beloved team was Rupp's Runts of 1965-66, featuring a starting five of Louie Dampier, Pat Riley, Larry Conley, Tommy Kron, and Thad Jaracz. With no starter taller than six-foot-five, the Runts used speed and high scoring to blaze a path of victory all the way to the NCAA championship game with Texas Western. There the odyssey ended, and the Wildcats came up short in a historic contest. Here is a glimpse of their style of play, with Conley (40) leading a fast break in the Coliseum and looking ahead for Dampier. Jaracz fills the lane to the left, while Kron does the same on the right. Out of the scene is Riley, who may have snatched the rebound and whipped an outlet pass to Conley, a commonplace act that memorable year. [Author's note - This was the team that made a Kentucky basketball fan out of my father, a transplanted Missourian.]

Above right: Despite their painful loss in the NCAA final, Rupp's Runts were welcomed home by an appreciative gathering of about 5,000 supporters in the Coliseum. Larry Conley and Tommy Kron addressed the assembly on behalf of the players, and after the ceremony hundreds of people came onto the floor to get autographs from the team. Here, Louie Dampier signs for young fans who still believe the Wildcats are number one.

The Committee of 101

Late in the 1965-66 season of Rupp's Runts, a hundred and one employees of Lexington's IBM plant each chipped in a few cents to send a telegram of encouragement to Coach Rupp and the Wildcats on the road. Within days, some of the group officially formed a club to support the basketball team and named themselves The Committee of 101. With Rupp's blessing and encouragement, they took on the role of program boosters that very season. They greeted the team at the airport on their return from their remaining road trips and sponsored The Committee of 101 Award for the Wildcats' assist leader at the postseason team banquet. The next year, they added ushering duties at Memorial Coliseum, a role that local Boy Scout troops had filled since the days of Alumni Gym. The Committee's first uniform was a dark blue coat, which was later changed to the current shade of royal blue after the move to Rupp Arena in 1976. The Committee of 101 is going strong today with over three hundred members, still ushering as "Blue Coats" for UK basketball, football, and other sports. Over the years the group has engaged in many charitable endeavors, including sponsoring and coaching a Junior Pro basketball team for young players.

Above left: Gene Oakley wears a modern model of the "Blue Coat" for the Committee of 101. In 2024, the longest tenured members of the Committee were Gene Oakley, Rex Payne, and David Trosper, all of whom joined in 1967 and had reached fifty-seven years of membership.

Above right: A closeup view of Oakley's jacket, with name badge and Committee patch.

Rupp in His Lair

Below left: A view of Adolph Rupp's desk in his Coliseum office with an unidentified man, circa 1966. (The film canisters stacked on the right front of the desk are marked as game film from the NCAA semi-final victory that year over Duke, 83-79.) The coach's workplace was in the very middle of the lower west wing of the building, with windows looking onto Lexington Avenue. The wall to the left is covered with pictures of the coach with various personalities and groups from throughout his career. His other office walls were also nearly covered with plaques, team pictures, Shriner certificates, and even portraits of Rupp's prize Hereford cows from his farm. Rupp's previous office in Alumni Gymnasium had been little more than a cramped cubicle, and he eagerly took advantage of the Coliseum's larger space to display his personal mementos on every available square inch. In the late 1940s, football coach Paul Bryant had occupied an Alumni Gymnasium office that was larger than—and adjacent to—Rupp's. According to Bryant, he could clearly hear much that was said by the vocal Rupp next door, including his exclamations to visiting recruits that they "had just walked into the pearly gates of basketball." When the Coliseum opened in 1950, the architectural plans again placed Bryant next to Rupp, this time in rooms of identical size. Bryant wrote that he soon moved to an office further away to gain more peace and quiet.

Below right: Another look at the same corner of Rupp's Coliseum office, circa 1967. He stands next to Felix Thurston, who was visiting the campus as a highly recruited high school senior from Owensboro, Kentucky. Rupp had recruited his first Black athlete for UK in 1964, Louisville's Wes Unseld, a future NBA star. But Unseld declined to be the program's first African American, and Rupp continued to unsuccessfully recruit top Black players within the state for several years. He was focused on signing a "Jackie Robinson-type" ground breaker, who would be a model student and a top athlete. In 1967, Thurston verbally committed to play for Kentucky, but eventually changed his mind and enrolled at Trinity University in Texas. It would be two more years before Tom Payne of Louisville accepted a varsity scholarship and became the first Black player for Rupp in 1970.

Big Blue on the Airwaves

For those unable to attend the men's games at Memorial Coliseum, they could still follow every contest on the radio. From its opening, the arena was home to multiple Kentucky radio announcers who described the games for their remote audiences. For many years, there was no single broadcaster and any station who registered with the University and paid a modest fee (initially $30-$80 per station per game, depending on the power of the radio tower transmitter) could cover the football and basketball schedules. The two most popular sportscasters were Claude Sullivan, who assembled a multi-station network sponsored by Standard Oil, and Cawood Ledford on the 50,000-watt Louisville-based WHAS. In 1965, Sullivan began announcing Cincinnati Reds games as well, but tragically died of cancer in late 1967. The next year UK consolidated its sports radio rights, and Ledford was selected to call both football and basketball games as the official "Voice of the Wildcats." Pictured here are some sample ads from basketball game programs over the years that touted a spectrum of UK radio coverage.

Top left: An ad in a February 1958 game program for the WHAS broadcast team of Cawood Ledford and Dave Martin.

Top right: WVLK's duo of Bill Sorrell and Ted Grizzard from a January 1964 program.

Bottom left: Mark "Boom-Boom" Halleck called games over WBLG and enjoyed exclusive post-game interviews with Rupp at courtside for a time. This announcement is from February 1965.

Bottom right: Jim Host announced Wildcat contests for several stations and networks, beginning with UK's own WBKY as a student in 1955. His subsequent career in business, politics, and civic service created a lasting legacy in Lexington, the Commonwealth, and throughout the country. For years he served as the play-by-play man for UK basketball on networks originating from WLAP and WVLK, and had the sad duty of announcing the death of Claude Sullivan, one of his radio mentors, during a live game broadcast in December 1967. Here he partners with George Conley, an SEC game official and father of star Wildcat Larry Conley, in a February 1965 ad.

The First Great Voice of the Wildcats

Claude Sullivan began announcing Wildcat basketball games full time over the radio in 1947, during the era of the Fabulous Five and at the tender age of twenty-two. He won every Kentucky Sportscaster of the Year award from its inception in 1959 through his final full year at the microphone in 1966. He was runner-up to Lindsey Nelson for National Sportscaster of the Year in 1960.

Below left: Claude Sullivan interviews Adolph Rupp after a Coliseum matchup with Tulane to end the 1965-66 regular season. The Kentucky coach consults a satisfying stat sheet following the 103-74 victory. As the dean of UK sportscasters at this point in his career, Sullivan had the privilege of calling games from a seat at the halfcourt line.

When Sullivan's two sons reached their teenage years in the mid-1960s, they joined him on press row. Older son David served as the broadcast engineer beside Sullivan in the Coliseum. Alan, the younger son, kept game statistics and distributed them to his father and others in the media. David later played varsity football for UK, while Alan studied architecture at the University.

Below right: Claude Sullivan broadcast his Kentucky basketball games solo. This game program ad is from 1966-67, his final season announcing UK basketball. During this time, he was also the play-by-play announcer for Kentucky football and the Cincinnati Reds. Sullivan passed away from cancer at the young age of forty-two.

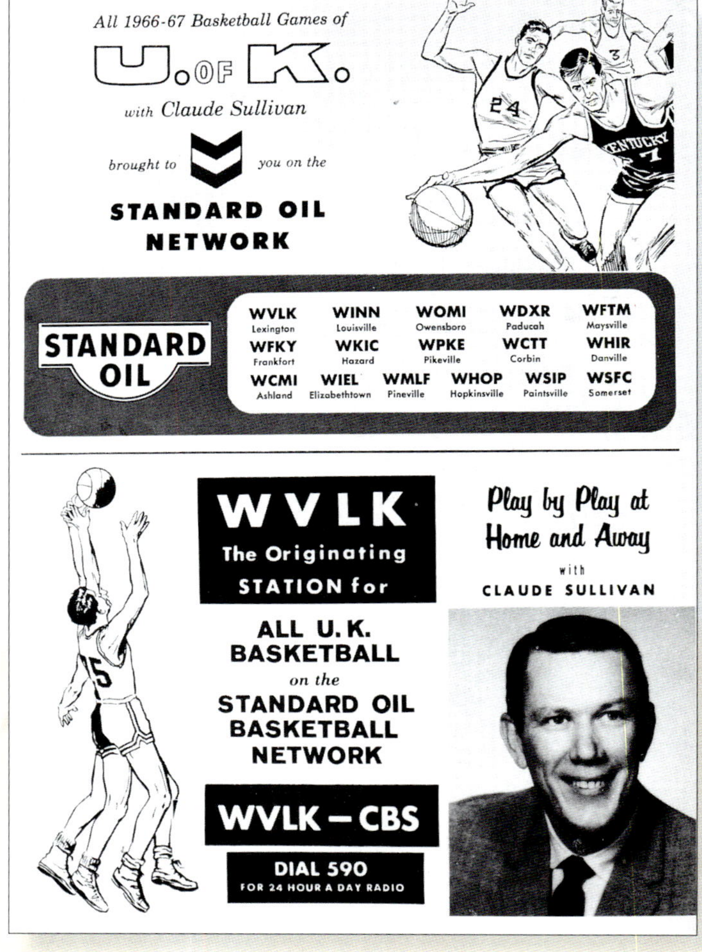

More Wildcat Voices

Top: Pictured here is a treasured possession owned by many Big Blue fans of the past. In 1969, the Committee of 101 worked with Cawood Ledford to produce an LP record of historical Kentucky basketball highlights. These were taken from archived radio broadcasts by Ledford and the late Claude Sullivan, with Coach Rupp offering commentary. Proceeds went to a scholarship fund administered by the 101, with the first copy of the record presented to Claude Sullivan's widow, Alyce.

Bottom: Adolph Rupp works as a one-time color man for play-by-play announcer Ralph Hacker. The occasion was likely the UKIT of December 1971, to which Colorado State sent its basketball team but not its home radio crew. Instead, the school arranged for Hacker to do the broadcast for their network. As Hacker called the action, Coach Rupp, whose team would play in the next game that night, asked if he could sit in and offer the color commentary. The Baron fulfilled this duty until having to leave late in the contest to prepare his own team.

Hacker had a long and highly distinguished career as a Kentucky sports broadcaster. After starting in radio by announcing high school sports and UK freshmen basketball games, he joined Cawood Ledford as color man in 1972 for Wildcat football and basketball games. Twenty years later, Ledford stepped down and Hacker took over the play-by-play role for both sports. When he retired from radio in 2001, he had served as the voice of Wildcat basketball for nearly a decade.

Signs of Change

Below left: On December 11, 1968, about forty Black UK students picketed outside Memorial Coliseum in protest of Kentucky's all-white team. Their signs called on the school to integrate the Wildcats, a goal that Coach Adolph Rupp had already been pursuing for several years. Darryl Bishop, although attending UK on a football scholarship, became the first African American to suit up for Kentucky basketball when he played on the freshmen team of 1969-70. At the time, first year students were not allowed by the NCAA to play varsity.

Below right: A year later, Tom Payne joined the Wildcats as the school's first African American player on the varsity. Here, he elevates above the rim against DePaul in the 1970 UKIT. His UK teammates, left to right, are Kent Hollenbeck (32), Tom Parker, Larry Stamper, and Mike Casey. After a single season, Payne left UK and signed an NBA contract. In Rupp's last year, 1971-72, Bishop and Elmore Stephens, another Black football player, joined the basketball team as walk-ons for part of the schedule. When Joe B. Hall took over as head coach in 1972-73, he signed Reggie Warford from Drakesboro, Kentucky. Four years later, Warford became the first African American in the basketball program to graduate.

A Title That Got Away

This picture represents, as much as any other in the UK photographic archives, what might have been. In 1966-67, as the Kentucky varsity struggled through Coach Rupp's worst season with a record of 13-13, the freshmen team built great hopes for the years to come. The stellar class included future All-Americans Dan Issel and Mike Pratt, but the brightest star was initially Mike Casey, a six-foot-four shooting guard out of Simpsonville, Kentucky. In the trio's first varsity season as sophomores, he averaged twenty points per game. The following year, Issel surpassed him as a scorer, and national championship hopes were thick in the Lexington air prior to the group's senior year of 1969-70. In the below photo taken as sophomores or juniors, Casey, Issel, and Pratt pose left to right with Rupp. In his fortieth campaign, the Baron would get another strong crack at an NCAA title. Tragically, in the summer prior to his senior season, Casey broke a leg in a car accident and was forced to sit out the year. The Wildcats still powered through their schedule with a hurricane of points and held the number one national ranking for much of the season before falling to Jacksonville in an NCAA regional final. (Jacksonville, with Artis Gilmore at center, went on to lose to UCLA in the finals.) Casey would return as a fifth-year senior in 1970-71 and average a solid seventeen points per game, but his speed and mobility were not what they had been. If it wasn't for his broken leg, another championship banner could very well be hanging in Rupp Arena today.

The Game Experience

Above left: The Wildcats take their pre-game free throws in the Coliseum during the 1968-69 season. At the line standing left-to right are Mike Pratt (22), Mike Casey (34), and Dan Issel (44). The Wildcats' warmup jackets of the 1960s, as seen here, were of unadorned white cotton with only "Kentucky" stitched on the back. They were far removed from the flamboyant, two-tone silk attire of the 1940s and 1950s.

Above right: As always, the stands are filling early. Students typically lined up well before gametime to grab a free – but limited – spot in the eastern stands on bench-type seating. For the most anticipated contests, students were allowed to stand in the corners and sit on the floor immediately in front of the first row of box seats at floor level, as seen in this image from the 1968-69 campaign. In the late 1960s, Kentucky games were still largely dress-up affairs. The UK ticket committee determined in the mid-1960s that standing room would no longer be permitted for the general public at basketball games. However, students would continue to be allowed to stand or sit wherever they could find space once their designated bleacher seats were all taken. Sometimes, students didn't completely claim their roughly 4,500 ticket allotment. When that occurred, and with five minutes until game time, civilians waiting in line at the outside ticket windows could purchase them.

A Millenary Milestone

Below left: Adolph Rupp walks from his team's bench as the crowd begins to celebrate the program's 1,000th all-time victory, the most in college basketball, on January 11, 1969. The scoreboard shows the final score over Florida, 88-67. Although Kentucky claimed this game for that impressive landmark of triumphs, the NCAA did not fully accept the school's documented list of wins. Over the years, further research and back-and-forth communications between UK and the NCAA have resulted in the team's current officially-recognized 1,000th win as occurring two games later against Tennessee. But on this night, Coach Rupp's view on the accounting of conquests was clear: "As long as we've got 'em, we're going to celebrate 'em." The location of the Wildcat bench was new that season, having been moved to the sideline from underneath the north basket, where it had been since the Coliseum opened. The change may have occurred because earlier in the decade the NCAA had finally lifted its rule against in-game coaching from the bench (outside of timeouts). Rupp was now positioned near mid-court and able to yell instructions to any point on the floor.

Below right: The 1,000th win for the Kentucky program was celebrated with a very large sheet cake. Members of the UK Athletics Board all lent a hand in lighting 1,000 individual candles on the dessert as the players stood by ready to eat. The candles created such a collective blaze that the confectionary soon started to melt. The entire Wildcat squad rushed in to save the day by blowing out the flames as the crowd roared. In the photo, Dan Issel stands tall in the left background while his teammates extinguish the fires. Similar baked cakes had been brought onto the court to commemorate other special basketball victories in the Coliseum.

A Heritage of Kentucky Basketball

Three generations of the Rupp family are represented here as Coach Adolph Rupp takes the hand of his young grandson, Chip (Adolph Rupp III), and guides him onto the Coliseum playing floor. The occasion is a post-game celebration of the Baron's 800th career victory on February 1, 1969, over Vanderbilt by a score of 103 - 89. Standing in the background on the far left is Esther Rupp, the wife of Adolph, and to her immediate left is their son, Herky (Adolph Rupp II). Visible over Herky's left shoulder is Joe B. Hall, the assistant coach who would eventually take the reins of the Kentucky program. Coach Rupp was a devoted family man who doted on his only son and grandchildren. Adolph had made sure that Herky received the honor of making the unofficial first basket in Memorial Coliseum prior to the Wildcats' inaugural practice there in 1950. A few years from this scene, Adolph would take Chip to the Wildcat's initial practice in Rupp Arena in October 1976, where the youngster would sink the first shot in that new arena. Thus, the Rupp family has put its personal stamp on all three of UK's main home courts: Alumni Gymnasium, Memorial Coliseum, and Rupp Arena.

Not So Happy

Albert B. "Happy" Chandler was a two-time governor of Kentucky, the commissioner of Major League Baseball when it was racially integrated by Jackie Robinson in 1947, and a passionate fan of UK basketball. His first governorship began in 1936 and he immediately supported the school's efforts to finance a fieldhouse, a project that came to fruition a decade later in the form of Memorial Coliseum. Chandler was a good friend of Adolph Rupp and one of the few public figures allowed to observe his practices, although he was reportedly thrown out of at least one session by the Baron for making too much noise. His son, Dan, was a bench warmer for Rupp in the mid-1950s. In the above photographs, Chandler's fiery support for Kentucky is evident as he rises to protest perceived injustices done to his Wildcats in Memorial Coliseum by a referee in 1970. His rooting passion for the Wildcats is unaffected by the amused and curious looks of those around him.

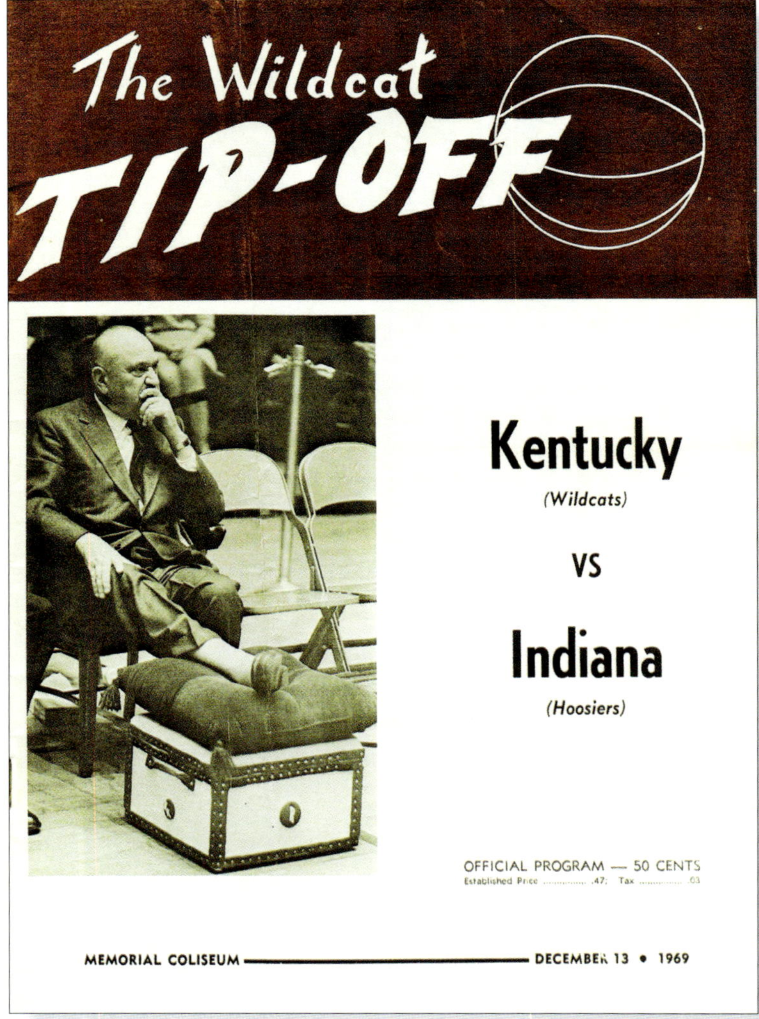

Trying Times

Above left: The 1968-69 and 1969-70 seasons were physically trying for Coach Rupp, who suffered from a foot infection resulting from diabetes complications. He had to sit for many of the games and practices with his leg supported. To increase his comfort, UK fans gave him a thick blue cushion and a footlocker on which to prop his leg. For games at the Coliseum, he also sat in a wooden armchair rather than on one of the metal folding chairs that made up the rest of the team "bench."

Above right: Rupp's public predicament was even immortalized on the cover of a UK game program in January 1969.

Wildcat without Equal

Top: All-American Dan Issel shoots from the outside against Georgia during another Wildcat triumph in February 1970. Looking on are fellow Wildcats (left to right) Tom Parker (12), Terry Mills, and Kent Hollenbeck. For some reason Kentucky sports their blue uniforms, which are normally worn in away games. Issel still holds the season and all-time UK men's scoring records, on his way to stellar careers in both the ABA and NBA pro leagues. At the end of his playing days, he was inducted into the Naismith Memorial Basketball Hall of Fame. For many UK fans, the debate over who is the greatest basketball Wildcat of them all begins and ends with Dan Issel.

Bottom: Issel anchored the 1969-70 Wildcats team that reached the number one ranking in the nation, a notable achievement during the era of UCLA's dynasty. From left, a pregame huddle from that season consists of Jim Dinwiddie, Terry Mills (father of future Wildcat Cameron Mills), Issel, Mike Pratt, and Larry Steele. Steele played nine years for the Portland Trail Blazers of the NBA, who honored him by retiring his uniform number.

Fire Away

Pete Maravich launches a jumper over the onrushing Dan Issel in their final matchup in Lexington in 1970. Memorial Coliseum has seen many outstanding athletes in its long history, but none greater than Dan Issel and Pete Maravich. "Pistol Pete," of the LSU Tigers, set the season and career NCAA Division 1 scoring records for men's basketball. He dribbled and passed like a Harlem Globetrotter, intentionally putting on a show for the crowd. His team never beat the Wildcats in six tries (freshmen could not play on the varsity then), but in the three seasons that he visited Lexington, tickets to the Coliseum were hard to come by. Appreciative Kentucky fans would yell "shoot!" when he crossed half court with the ball. Maravich never disappointed, firing away from any distance despite no three-point line or shot clock being in effect at the time. He had the full support of his head coach, who also happened to be his father.

In his first Coliseum appearance, Maravich poured in forty-four points (equaling his average) but needed thirty-eight shots to get there. Meanwhile, Issel's twenty-one points led the victorious Wildcats. Coach Rupp seemed content to let the Pistol get his points as long as his teammates were well-defended. The next year in Lexington, Maravich shot even more, totaling forty-five points on fifty-three attempts. Issel increased his output to thirty-six points and UK won again. The prolific scorers met a final time in Memorial as seniors in 1970, and they put on an offensive exhibition. The largest crowd in the history of the Coliseum - 13,690 - jammed the arena for the unforgettable shootout. Maravich set Memorial's single game record with an amazing fifty-five points, scoring and passing like a magician. He surpassed the Coliseum record of fifty-one points by Cliff Hagan, set against Temple on December 5, 1953. Issel took half as many shots as Maravich, but still rang up thirty-five efficient points in another Kentucky victory. Midway through the second half, Maravich passed Elvin Hayes' career point total to move into second place on the all-time NCAA scoring list. When the arena PA announcer informed the crowd of this feat, Rupp loudly complained to those around him, "Why in the hell do they have to announce that?" Both Issel and Maravich would later be inducted into the Naismith Memorial Basketball Hall of Fame, and their like would never be seen again on the floor of the Coliseum.

Rupp's Final Staff

A stern-looking Adolph Rupp poses with his staff in Memorial Coliseum during his final season of 1971-72. From left stand Dick Parsons, Joe B. Hall, Rupp, and Gale Catlett. The Baron had assured Hall several years before that when he retired, Hall would be promoted to head coach. However, during this final season, Rupp seemed at times to be backing Catlett as his successor. Of course, Hall ultimately won the position and led UK to the 1978 NCAA national championship and two more Final Fours. Coach Parsons remained a highly valuable assistant to Hall for eight years. Parsons had played varsity basketball and baseball (a sport in which he was an All-American in 1961) for Kentucky, and had coached the Wildcats' baseball team in the early 1970s. With Hall's hiring as head coach, Catlett accepted the top job at the University of Cincinnati and began a long and successful career leading the Cincinnati Bearcats and the West Virginia Mountaineers.

Jim Andrews Versus the Evil Orange

Jim Andrews was an All-SEC center that bridged the coaching eras of Adolph Rupp and Joe B. Hall. In this picture he lofts one of the most famous shots in Memorial Coliseum history. In January 1972, Tennessee came to Lexington with their usual talented team that was again challenging UK for SEC preeminence. The Volunteer's pregame warmup routine under coach Ray Mears ran like a circus act, with fancy dribbling and passing in the layup line. A Tennessee unicyclist rode around the periphery, a spectacle that was cheered at home in Knoxville and jeered heartily in the Coliseum. Students had waited in line for hours to get the best seats for the showdown, and the campus cafeteria had supplied the queue with healthy orange slices (the same vibrant hue as the hated Tennessee's school color). Now the orange pieces came flying onto the arena floor as the students aimed for the Volunteers. The start of the game was delayed as the smeared fruit was cleaned from the court. Then the hard-fought clash on the court began. With a few seconds left the score was tied, 70-70, and Kentucky held the ball. In a time-out huddle, the UK coaches called a play for Andrews down low and he responded, hitting this floater to win it. Andrews' basket as well as another Kentucky victory in Knoxville gave UK the head-to-head tiebreaker with Tennessee for the SEC title and the conference's lone NCAA tournament bid. (There was no SEC tournament during this period, and until the 1974-75 season, only one team from each conference was allowed to play in the NCAA tournament.)

Leaving the Limelight

Top right: Adolph Rupp steps into his own spotlight at his final home game as Kentucky's head coach on March 6, 1972, at the request of Athletic Director Harry Lancaster, his former longtime assistant coach. Earlier, when Rupp had first walked onto the court before the game, the UK band had collectively called out, as it always did, "Hello, Adolph!" Although his retirement was not yet official as he sought to continue coaching past the mandatory state employee's retirement age of seventy, most observers knew that his career was ending.

Bottom: After easily defeating Auburn, Rupp was honored at midcourt with a standing ovation, surrounded by most of the twenty-two living All-Americans that he had produced. These included such past stars as Forest "Aggie" Sale, Carey Spicer, Ellis Johnson, Alex Groza, Ralph Beard, Bill Spivey, Cliff Hagan, Frank Ramsey, Cotton Nash, Louie Dampier, and Dan Issel. To mark the occasion, Rupp gave each former Wildcat an autographed photo of himself.

A Big Change

Adolph Rupp and Joe B. Hall share a moment prior to Hall's first game as Kentucky's head coach on December 4, 1972. The Baron holds a funnel of popcorn that he will soon enjoy from his seat in the Coliseum stands, while Joe B. holds a rolled-up program, his signature game prop. The Hall era got off to a rough start as the Wildcats lost to Iowa. Rupp retained his office in the Coliseum's lower level as well as his radio and television shows that first year, all of which kept the pressure on Hall. Still, the new coach managed to guide Kentucky to an SEC title and NCAA tournament berth.

Quiet but Intense

Whether under Adolph Rupp or Joe B. Hall, UK basketball practices in the Coliseum were intense and focused, with no extraneous sounds allowed unless, in the words of Rupp, one could "improve upon the silence." Here, the Wildcats go five-on-five in Hall's first season, with starters in white jerseys and reserves in dark.

The Final Storm

This image is another example of Kentucky fans "storming" the court after a special Wildcat win. This spontaneous celebration occurred on March 8, 1973, and it capped Joe B. Hall's first season as UK's head coach. Despite the immense pressures of succeeding Adolph Rupp at the head of the men's basketball program, the first such coaching change in forty-two years, Hall led his team to an SEC championship in an era when only the conference winner was allowed to advance to the NCAA tournament. This winner-take-all showdown was with the Tennessee Volunteers, both teams sporting a 13-4 conference record. Kentucky came out on top, 86-81. As joyous students ran onto the floor, the players hoisted Hall up high, where he flashed a "V" for victory. It appears that this was the last time to date that UK fans have rushed the court. For Hall, the conference title in his first year at the helm of the Wildcats proved that he was the rightful successor to the long legacy of Coach Adolph Rupp.

Joe B. Hall's Coaching Legacy

Coach Joe B. Hall's coaching staff for his third season was groundbreaking. In the combined portrait below are coaches (left to right) Dick Parsons, Joe B. Hall, Lynn Nance, and Leonard Hamilton. Veteran assistant coach Parsons had been with Hall from the beginning, while assistants Nance and Hamilton were new additions to the program for the 1974-75 campaign. Hamilton was the first African American coach for Kentucky basketball, and he immediately made an impact with his recruitment of Jack Givens and James Lee from local Lexington high schools. Hamilton remained at UK until Hall retired in 1986, then moved on to head coaching positions at Oklahoma State University, the University of Miami, the Washington Wizards of the NBA, and Florida State University. As of the 2024-25 season, he has led the FSU basketball team for 23 years.

Super Southpaw

In Memorial Coliseum's latter years as the home of UK men's basketball, Kevin Grevey shone brightly as a left-handed, sharpshooting, All-American forward. Here he drives aggressively against Vanderbilt. NCAA rules at the time of his enrollment prevented first-year players from competing on varsity teams. Instead, Grevey was joined on the UK freshman squad with other talented athletes like Jimmy Dan Conner, Mike Flynn, and Bob Guyette. The underclassmen won all twenty-two games on their schedule in 1971-72, many of them by over forty points, and entered Kentucky basketball lore as the "Super Kittens." UK fans fully expected a national championship from them in the future. The next year was Joe B. Hall's first as head coach, and Grevey's gang moved up to the varsity. The Wildcats won the conference title before losing in the second round of the NCAA tourney. The following season of 1973-74 was disastrous, as UK limped to a 13-13 record. The former Super Kittens had one last chance to fulfill their varsity promise. To add skill and depth on the inside, Hall brought in freshmen bruisers Mike Phillips and Rick Robey, as well as forwards Jack Givens and James Lee. The Wildcats of 1974-75 took off like a rocket, finishing with a record of 26-5 and reaching the NCAA finals. It all ended in a heartbreaker, as the Cats lost to UCLA and Coach John Wooden in his last game, 92-85. Grevey and his fellow Super Kittens, however, had earned a lasting place in the pantheon of unforgettable Kentucky teams twice over.

Banners Abundant

Kentucky and Georgia fight for the opening tip of the second half of their matchup on February 8, 1975. Jumping for the Wildcats is freshman center Rick Robey, number 53. Also on the court for Kentucky, all of them seniors, are All-American forward Kevin Grevey (on the far left and partially hidden by the referee), forward Bob Guyette (45), guard Jimmy Dan Conner (20), and his backcourt mate, Mike Flynn (24). Prominent in the background of the photo are the large championship banners listing SEC and NCAA titles. These covered the windows of glass blocks high above the court. This was the first season that the banners were hung, a feature that would be carried over to Rupp Arena when it opened in 1976. Below the banners are the temporary bleachers that accommodated about 250 Kentucky legislators and their guests, as well as a fronting table for the media.

Celebrating Another Final Four

The 1974-75 Wildcats are greeted by a Coliseum crowd after their return from defeating Indiana - formerly ranked number one in the nation and unbeaten – in the NCAA Mideast Regional finals. The team is decked out in their mod travel attire of turtlenecks and blue-and-white-checkered sportscoats, very much in style that year. They would soon be on their way to the NCAA semi-finals in San Diego (now known as the Final Four), where they would beat Syracuse handily before losing to UCLA. It was Coach John Wooden's final game and tenth national championship. The freshmen stars of that team, Jack "Goose" Givens, James Lee, Mike Phillips, and Rick Robey, learned from the hard loss and brought home another NCAA title to Lexington as seniors in 1978.

Colonels in the Coliseum

For two memorable years, Memorial Coliseum featured both collegiate and professional basketball action on its hardwood. The Kentucky Colonels had been an original franchise of the American Basketball Association (ABA) when it was founded in 1967. The professional league competed with the established National Basketball Association (NBA) for a decade before it disbanded and four of its teams joined the NBA. Over its history, ABA teams came and went with dizzying regularity, but the Colonels thrived from its home base of Freedom Hall in Louisville. By the 1970s, Colonels owners John Y. Brown Jr. (Kentucky Fried Chicken magnate and future Kentucky state governor) and his wife, Ellie Brown, sought to capitalize on their team's duo of former UK All-Americans, Louie Dampier and Dan Issel, by playing a few annual dates in Lexington at Memorial Coliseum. The Colonels were allowed to schedule four games in the Coliseum during the 1973-74 campaign and six contests there in 1974-75, but they could not be played during the Wildcats' home season. The agreement was not renewed, and although there were serious efforts to have the Colonels return to Lexington once Rupp Arena was scheduled to open in late 1976, the ABA and Colonels folded before this could become a reality.

Below left: Louie Dampier puts up a running shot in a Coliseum battle with the Utah Stars. Dampier signed with the Colonels straight from college, and played in the ABA every year of its existence. One of the ABA's innovations was the three-point field goal from beyond twenty-two feet and nine inches from the basket, which was custom made for Dampier's long-range accuracy. He set the ABA record for most three-point shots made in a season and career, as well as the most games played in league history, all of which led to his induction into the Naismith Memorial Basketball Hall of Fame.

Below right: The dynamic Julius "Dr. J" Erving of the New York Nets looks to drive on the Colonel's Marv Roberts in the Coliseum. Erving won MVP awards in both the ABA and NBA, and was the most dynamic offensive force in professional basketball during the 1970s.

Historical Cover

To commemorate the final men's home game at Memorial Coliseum on March 8, 1976, a special game program was produced with a cover illustrating the basketball program's three main home courts, including the newly-built Rupp Arena. Inside, a special section documented the highlights of the Wildcats' years in the Coliseum, with memories of special players and events. It was a fitting souvenir for the capacity crowd of devoted Kentucky fans.

Too Close for Comfort

Below left: For the final men's game in Memorial Coliseum, Coach Joe B. Hall invited the retired Adolph Rupp to sit on the team bench one last time. Here, Truman Claytor is called forth by the PA announcer and receives encouragement from the two generations of UK coaching legends. Winning another SEC title and a ticket to the NCAA tournament was, unfortunately, out of the question that night for Kentucky against Mississippi State. Instead, the Wildcats needed a win simply to improve their record to 16-10 and pray for a spot in the lesser National Invitation Tournament (NIT).

Below right: Its "sitting room only" one last time as UK struggles mightily to put away Mississippi State in their Coliseum curtain call. Twenty-six years before, only a furious Kentucky comeback had kept Vanderbilt from spoiling the final game down the street at Alumni Gymnasium. Now, UK found itself down by seven points with only 1:23 left, with no shot clock or three-point field goal then in effect. Even the normally optimistic Cawood Ledford, "The Voice of the Wildcats," lamented to his radio listeners, "Kentucky has gone down in flames." During a time-out, State player Joe Dean Jr. yelled over the Bulldogs' radio network, "Hey Mom, we won!" It was loud enough to be heard over the Kentucky network as well, whose microphones were nearby. (A few years later, Dean would serve as an assistant coach on Joe B. Hall's UK staff.) But the Wildcats pulled off another Coliseum miracle, with Jack Givens hitting a tying basket just before the buzzer, forcing overtime. Kentucky would not be denied, finally winning, 94-93, and prompting Rupp to exclaim, "That's a helluva way to treat an old man!" The win earned UK an NIT invitation, and they took four more games in New York City to claim that national tournament's crown.

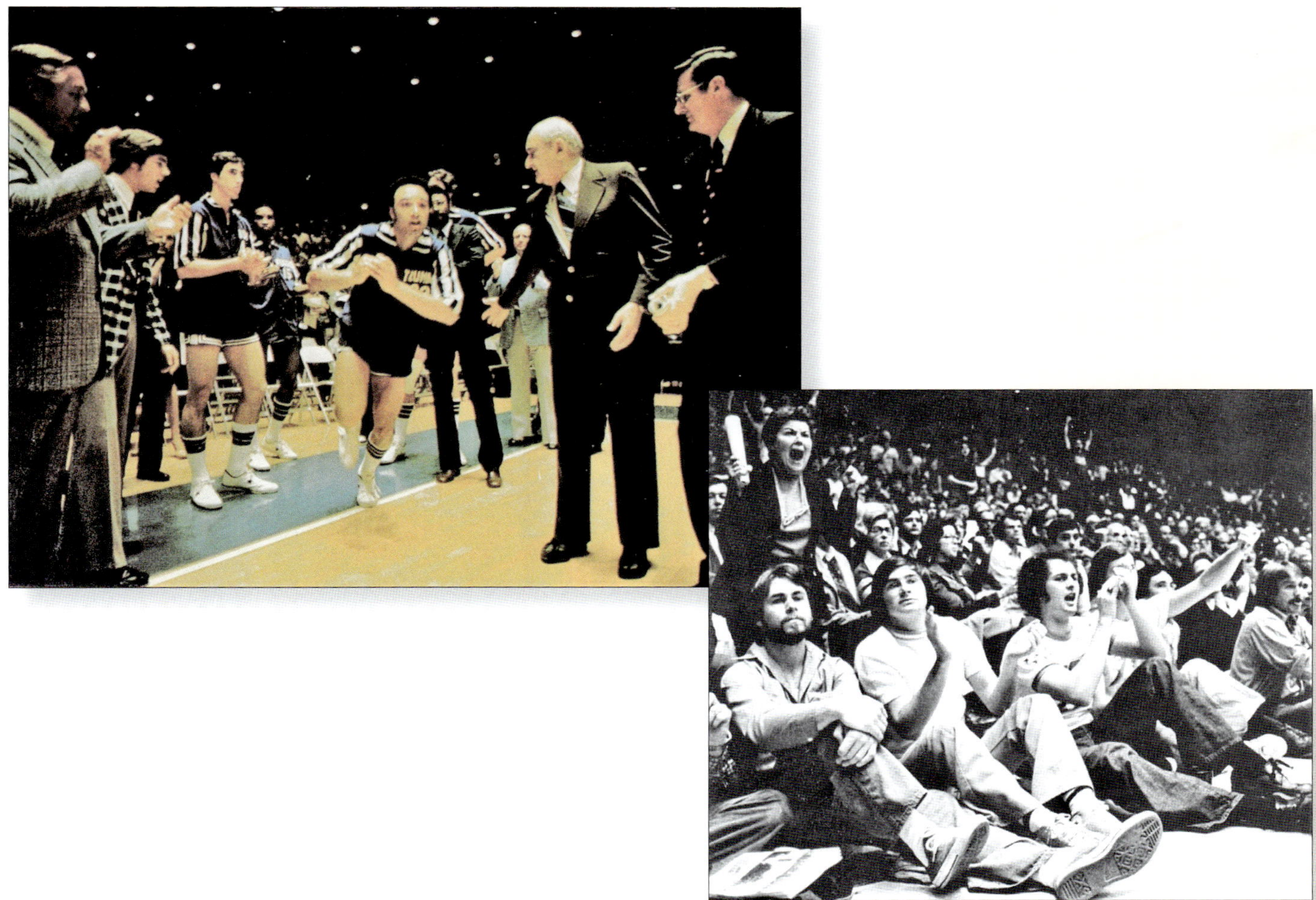

Madness in Memorial

After the Wildcat men moved their games to Rupp Arena, they continued to use the Coliseum for most of their practices and for two public exhibitions in the early 1990s. In a strange twist of events, the men were forced to return to the Coliseum for a final competitive matchup in the 2009 NIT. Kentucky had failed to be selected for the NCAA tournament that year but was tapped to host a first round NIT contest against the University of Nevada, Las Vegas. Since Rupp Arena was already booked for the boys' Sweet Sixteen tournament, the Wildcats hosted their game in Memorial and beat UNLV, 70-60.

Another annual event where UK fans could cheer on the men in the Coliseum was Midnight Madness (held every October 15–or thereabouts—and just after 12:00 a.m.). This spectacle was begun in 1982 by Coach Joe B. Hall and marked the team's first practice of the season. It took a few years for the "Midnight Madness" moniker to be officially chosen. It didn't take long for Madness to attract overflowing throngs to the Coliseum. The annual kickoff was relabeled "Big Blue Madness" in 2000.

Top right: Some fans camped out for several days to ensure they could claim a free ticket for the event. Here, tents have been set up by early arrivals at a back corner of Memorial in the mid-1990s. The Joe Craft Center would be added to this area of the building a decade later.

Bottom right: Keth Bogans moves through the crowd as he follows the arena steps down to the court during the Madness introductions, circa 2002. The women's team joined the annual festivities in the early 2000s. To accommodate more fans, the event was moved to Rupp Arena in 2005 and held earlier in the evening. While Rupp has almost twice the original capacity of Memorial Coliseum, many of the older Kentucky faithful still believe that the crowd atmosphere of the Coliseum was more electric for both Madness and the men's games.

Left: An energized crowd crams the Coliseum for the 1998 Madness.

Mister Wildcat

Middle right: Bill Keightley, long known as "Mr. Wildcat," stands in his personal domain of the Coliseum equipment storage room in 1992. Keightley was the beloved equipment manager for the men's basketball program for well over forty years. In 1962, he was working as a mail carrier in Lexington when George Hukle, a fellow postal worker and the UK basketball equipment manager, hired him as assistant equipment manager. A decade later, he took over Hukle's spot while still delivering mail for a time. For generations of Wildcat basketball players under six head coaches, Keightley was a trusted father figure who could encourage them after a coach's dressing down or a bout of homesickness. He became such an integral part of the program that he was eventually given a spot on the Kentucky game bench beside the head coach. His retired jersey, bearing the number "48" for his years of service to the basketball program, hangs in the rafters of Rupp Arena, and he is a member of the Kentucky Athletic Hall of Fame. Since his passing in 2008, the spot on the Rupp Arena court in front of his former seat has been permanently marked with "Mr. Wildcat."

Bottom right: Karen Marlowe, daughter of Bill Keightley, stands outside the door to the "Bill Keightley Equipment Room," known informally as "The Cage," in 2023. Marlowe is a devoted employee for UK Athletics at the Coliseum.

Gradual Changes to the Coliseum

Top right: Beginning in 1990, the north endzone bleachers were remodeled into a two-story complex that housed weight training, lockers, and meeting rooms on the ground floor, with a reception area and offices above. This expanded the needed facilities for the sports programs sharing the Coliseum, but was also the first significant change to the original layout of the building. The later addition of the Joe Craft Center in 2007 incorporated this older space. The image shows this section of the Coliseum in 2023.

Bottom right: A view from inside the endzone complex prior to the addition of the Craft Center. The one-way windows of the team lounge and meeting room look out onto the Coliseum playing floor.

Left: In May of 2007, the playing floor of the Coliseum was replaced for the first time. Although much of the choicest areas of the court were carefully preserved by the University—such as the center jump circle and the spot of Vernon Hatton's miracle shot against LaSalle—most of it was unceremoniously ripped up and tossed into a dumpster in front of the arena. The wooden slats had originally been permanently attached to its concrete foundation, and the only way to remove them in a timely manner was to tear them up into jagged pieces. Word quickly spread of the historical contents of the dumpster, and by the end of the day hundreds of board feet had been scavenged by UK fans. Pictured at left is a piece from one of the original free throw lanes owned by Mike Murphy, who was a team manager for UK men's basketball, including the 1978 NCAA championship team. The slat is signed by members of the 1978 Wildcats.

Title IX Women's Sports and Swimming in the Coliseum

The Lady Kats and UK Hoops

As the Wildcat men's era in Memorial Coliseum wound down, new female tenants moved in. Federal Title IX legislation, passed in 1972, mandated (among other things) equality for men's and women's sports in institutions of education. For UK, this meant a gradual increase in the number of varsity sports for female athletes during the 1970s.

Between 1925 and 1974, there was no varsity women's basketball team at the University of Kentucky. However, the women's program was revived for the 1974-75 season and their inaugural team, then known as the Lady Kats, was coached by Sue Feamster and played in the Coliseum. They played a schedule largely filled with regional schools. However, the program was affiliated with the Association for Intercollegiate Athletics for Women (AIAW), which held a year-end national championship tournament. In UK's first year, the women made it to the quarterfinals of the regional competition for the AIAW title.

Above right: Kentucky's Cassie Cassinger puts up a shot against Morehead State University in the team's first year. In contrast with the more-celebrated men's team, the early Lady Kats did not even carry the "Kentucky" name on their jerseys.

Bottom right: By 1982, the women's level of play and uniform quality had vastly improved, and they were a member of the SEC, like the men. Here, star forward Valerie Still scores against Illinois. Still was an All-American and set the all-time UK women's scoring record at 2,763 points. She led the 1981-82 Lady Kats to their first SEC tournament title, and captained the 1982-83 team to its first SEC regular season championship.

Top: The women's basketball name was changed to Wildcats in 1995, and the program has since been rebranded as UK Hoops. Kentucky has reached the Elite Eight of the NCAA tournament four times, most recently in 2013. Above, DeNesha Stallworth goes for a rebound in November 2013.

Gymnastics

Bottom: The women's varsity gymnastics team was also inaugurated in 1974, with an initial home in the Seaton Center. It was several years before the team moved into Memorial Coliseum for their home meets. Here, senior Jackie Chatfield performs on the balance beam in 1983.

Top: One of the finest gymnasts ever to wear a Kentucky uniform was All-American Jenny Hanson. She won national awards for her skill on multiple apparatuses in the mid-1990s, and once scored a perfect 10.0 on the balance beam.

Bottom: Audrey Harrison leaps during her beam routine in 2012.

Volleyball

It took Kentucky women's volleyball a few years to join the other female varsity sports. Founded in 1977, the squad's original practice and competitive home was old Alumni Gymnasium, with the team moving to Memorial Coliseum for games in 1980. The volleyball program has reached the pinnacle of NCAA competition, winning a national title in the 2020 season (the finals were played in April 2021 due to the COVID-19 pandemic).

Top left: Kentucky's Sandy Glasscock spikes between the arms of her opponents in the Coliseum in 1982.

Top right: UK Senior Molly Dreisbach blocks the Minnesota Golden Gophers in 1995.

Bottom: Whitney Billings, a UK freshman, sets the ball against LSU in 2010.

Swimming and Diving

Swimming and diving were UK varsity sports for men in Memorial Coliseum from the very beginning. With women's teams added in 1983, the Coliseum remained the school's home for water sports until the Lancaster Aquatic Center opened on campus in 1988.

Top left: The interior of the Coliseum's pool wing just prior to its completion in 1950. The pool space was small, with seating limited to only a few hundred on tiered bleachers. Natural light was heavily filtered by the windows of glass blocks.

Top right: Looking like a spider-man stuck to the overhead, Steve Mitaskis of Georgia performs one of his winning dives at the 1952 SEC championships in the Coliseum. The athlete's shadow against the ceiling seems to indicate that he has little room for error, and his springboard maneuvers must have been carefully practiced.

Bottom: Senior Kim Gugino dives during the final season of water sports in 1987-88 at the Coliseum. The pool was eventually filled in to provide more space for administrative and classroom functions.

The Coliseum as Stage

Deep in the Coliseum

Beneath the Coliseum's stands on the western side were the many varsity athletic spaces that the general public did not see. Directly across from the offices of the athletic director and head football and basketball coaches was a sitting nook, where players, reporters, and others could wait to be seen. Here, footballers John Riggs (left), Harry Jones (center), and John Baldwin (right) crowd—and clown—onto one of the alcove's couches in January 1952. Standing behind them (left to right) are teammates Bob Fry, Frank Fuller, and Larry Jones. (Harry and Larry Jones were twins, and for a time wore games jersey numbers 1A and 1B, respectively, on the UK football team.) All were seniors on the 1952 squad. Strung high on the wall behind them are photos of past UK net stars. Out of sight in the adjacent main corridor were displayed photos of former football standouts as well. The lower corridors were built with the same golden cinder block walls and brown terrazzo floors as on the arena's upper levels. In later years, this nook was walled off into a separate space.

The Joys of Registration

Many students ended their years at Kentucky by receiving their diplomas in graduation ceremonies held in the Coliseum. Four years prior, most of these same scholars began their UK experience within the same building as they navigated the class registration process for the first time. This image is from the start of the Spring semester in 1952, when signing up for classes was done with pencil, paper, and not a little stress.

A Fine Concert Hall

Above left: An orchestra rehearses in the Coliseum, circa 1950, perhaps in preparation for a community concert as part of the facility's versatile function as a performing arts hall. The lower north bleachers, which were later removed in 1990 to add additional training and office space, are to the left. The exterior windows in that section of the arena, as well as those at the top of the other three sides of the building, served to create a somewhat open atmosphere during daylight. The Coliseum's original blueprints included fifty-foot-tall folding acoustic panels hanging from the ceiling. These were intended to be moved into different configurations to create concert spaces of various sizes and with exceptional sound quality. The massive sliding panels were to be stowed in the tall storage alcoves flanking both sides of the lobby doors. However, the panels were never installed, either because of cost and engineering challenges, or because the acoustic qualities of the arena were so good that they weren't necessary. The curved seating along the Coliseum's sides provided audience members a head-on view to the center of the large space, and the flat ceiling covered with acoustic panels helped to preserve an atmosphere of crisp and true sound. For concerts and talks, the stage could be oriented facing the west stands, or placed at the lobby end for maximum attendance of 10,000 or more, with folding chairs placed on the floor.

Above right: An example of the Coliseum arranged for a concert with the stage placed at the lobby end and all seating made available. An unidentified singer and pianist perform before a large crowd, circa 1955. This is one of many well-attended events open to the community as part of the Central Kentucky Concert and Lecture Series.

Hollywood Comes to Lexington

Hollywood star Bob Hope headlined the first annual Blue Grass Festival, a pre-Kentucky Derby extravaganza held at Memorial Coliseum on April 30, 1953. The festival's chairman was Hugh Meriwether, a member of the architectural team that designed Memorial Coliseum. The entertaining acts played before a crowd of 14,000 and helped raise money for cancer research in Kentucky. Other comedy routines, singers, and dancers shared the stage, with Hope closing the show with his signature song, "Thanks for the Memories." He is pictured off stage in one of the ready areas at the southern end of the arena. Hope returned to headline the festival in the Coliseum the following year, but for an attendance about half as strong. The festival lasted only one more year as a lead into the Kentucky Derby weekend, as ticket sales fell sharply again.

The Beer Barrel Heist

Once upon a time, the Kentucky-Tennessee footbal rivalry featured an annual trophy that was kept in the possession of each year's victor. This was the Beer Barrel, an oaken cask with opposite ends painted orange and blue to signify the competing schools' colors. The scoring result from each engagement was marked on its circumference. The barrel debuted in 1925 and was labeled as "Ice Water," a comic nod to the then-national prohibition on the production of non-medicinal alcohol. The Wildcats won the barrel that first year but rarely prevailed over the Volunteers in the coming seasons. But with Paul "Bear" Bryant as coach, UK beat the Vols in Lexington in 1953, 27-21, to regain the Beer Barrel. The container was then locked away in an equipment room of Memorial Coliseum for safe keeping. Within a week, the drum was gone, stolen by a group of UT fratentity boys impersonating UK alumni. Somehow, posing as interested recent "graduates," they conned a custodian into showing them the trophy's location. The thieves later claimed to have even run into Adolph Rupp in a Coliseum hallway and shared a brief conversation. After the janitor was gone, the Tennesseans managed to return to the locked room with bolt cutters and escape with the barrel in tow.

Below left: UK employees D.T. Doyle and George Erhart examine the cut chain to a lock on the door of the storage area. A few days later, three student leaders from Knoxville announced that in the spirit of goodwill they would return the barrel to Lexington. Assuring UK that they were not the perpetrators, the trio drove with the trophy in the trunk of a car to the front of the Coliseum, where a stage with microphones had been set up to celbrate its return.

Below right: Pictured with the barrel trophy are from left, probably Lucien Dale, a member of the UT student government, and Carter "Corky" Glass, student body president for UK. Several hundred students and local citizens attended the event, but Coach Bryant had already left for home, declaring, "I wouldn't dignify it by my appearance." The final season of the Beer Barrel was 1997, a Tennessee win. Just prior to the next year's game, a tragic automobile accident involving a drunk driver (who was a UK football player) and two deaths resulted in the permanent suspension of the barrel trophy due to its association with alcohol. The barrel is currently in the possession of Tennessee.

More Fallen Heros to Remember

Although Memorial Coliseum's original dedication was to the Kentucky fatalities of World War Two, it also has been re-consecrated periodically as a hall of honor for the state's war dead of subsequent military conflicts. This first occurred only a few years after the building opened, with the conclusion of the Korean War. Professor John Horine again hand-lettered individual names of the fallen heroes—1,159 of them—onto large sheets. These were hung in several frames mounted on the wall near the top of the western ramp leading to the concourse. The annual baccalaureate service for 800 UK graduates was held on Memorial Day of 1954. As in 1950, the program included observances in word and song of the state's recently lost soldiers, sailors, and Marines, with many of their families and friends in attendance. The service included a musical arrangement of "For the Fallen," as there had been in the 1950 Coliseum dedication. It ended with the somber playing of "Taps," the traditional close to the military workday and memorial ceremonies.

UNIVERSITY OF KENTUCKY

Baccalaureate Exercises

NINETEEN HUNDRED FIFTY-FOUR

Memorial Services

for

Kentucky's Korean War Dead

SUNDAY, MAY THE THIRTIETH

Memorial Coliseum

3:00 p.m. (Central Standard Time)

Lexington

Burgled Safe!

Anybody home? Sports Publicity Director Ken Kuhn looks into the safe opened by thieves when they broke into Memorial Coliseum ticket office Monday night. A loss of between $11,000 and $12,000 has been estimated.

Thieves Take $12,000 From Coliseum Safe

An unknown number of burglars chopped open a safe in the ticket office of Memorial Coliseum and stole about $12,000 Monday night following the UK-Auburn game.

The loss was estimated at between $11,000 and $12,000 by Bernie Shively, director of athletics. At least $5,000 of the stolen money was insured, Shively said. The money represented receipts from the Auburn game and from the sale of NCAA regional tournament tickets. No tickets were taken, he said—probably because they were locked in separate compartments.

UK police said the bills were not marked and the numbers were not recorded.

The burglary was reported about 7 o'clock Tuesday morning when Janitor Charlie Huglett found the door to the ticket office open. The cylinder, plate and lock had been removed in order to open the door.

The safe was found in a men's room near the office by Shively and a policeman. The safe, estimated to weigh about 2,000 pounds, had been wheeled into the wash room, where it had been chopped open. About $90 in silver was left in the office, Shively said.

The thieves cut through a layer of steel, three inches of insulating material and another layer of steel to reach the contents of the safe.

A soft drink machine and a candy machine were also forced open and a small amount of money removed. The offices of the building manager and the assistant coaches were opened, desks and two cabinets broken into, and $1.40 taken.

Police theorized that the thieves attended the game and remained hidden in the building until it was empty. Seth Taylor, UK chief of services, said that University police had checked the building at 11 o'clock and found everything normal. He added that a nationwide alarm had been put out for the burglars.

Police theorized the thieves, apparently amateurs, first broke into the coin machines and, when only about $12 was found, they located and hacked open the safe.

The offices were probably opened as an afterthought, police said.

There was no visible evidence of a forced entry into the Coliseum, the officers said, but a chain securing one of the rear doors had been twisted

(Continued on Page 16)

The Kentucky KERNEL

Vol. XLVIII University of Kentucky, Lexington, Ky., Friday, March 1, 1957 Number 17

Law Dean Resigns

By ANN SMITH

Elvis J. Stahr Jr. resigned as dean of the UK College of Law and University Provost this week to become vice chancellor of the University of Pittsburgh.

Dean Stahr has been on a leave of absence from the Uni-

The Case of the Burgled Coliseum

Above, the UK student newspaper, The Kentucky Kernel, reports big news in the case of a Memorial Coliseum heist. The arena's ticket office handled large sums of cash from game ticket sales, which were kept in a free-standing safe until the bills could be transferred to a bank. In February 1957, the ticket office was also processing advance ticket sales for the NCAA regional tournament which would be hosted by UK. On the evening of February 25, over $10,000 (equivalent to about $110,000 in inflation-adjusted dollars by 2024) was locked up in the Coliseum safe after the Wildcats easily defeated the Auburn Tigers at home. Once the arena was inspected and locked up by security at 11:00 pm, two robbers entered the building through an unlocked window. One of the burglars was twenty-seven-year-old William Sparks, who had recently been fired from his campus custodial job for suspected thievery. Sparks lived in a house on College View (a street that no longer exists) which backed directly onto an alleyway behind the Coliseum. His accomplice was Elmer Clem, his own stepfather. It's not clear whether the men knew about the unusually large treasure in the ticket office safe, and they began their hunt for money by prying open the concourse vending machines and ransacking the desks and cabinets of some offices. Finally, they broke into the ticket office, tipped over the 2,000-pound safe, and attacked it with an axe. Sparks and Clem managed to open the repository and left the Coliseum with its entire contents.

The next morning the crime was discovered, and the local police called in. Sparks was soon a suspect because the outdoor dogs of his neighbor, who seemed to bark at everything in sight, had not barked the night before, indicating that they must have been familiar with the perpetrators as they entered and left the nearby arena. Within days, Sparks was arrested when his large cash purchases aroused further suspicion. He also stated to police that he often chewed gum, and the brand of wrappers found in his yard matched the empty wrappers left at the crime scene. His stepfather, Elmer Clem, was picked up months later by police in Evansville, Indiana, and claimed that his share of the loot had been stolen from him by an assailant. Only a fraction of the stolen money was found, but insurance covered the loss.

Packing Them In

A packed Memorial Coliseum hosts a sock hop, with the basketball court serving as the dance floor. The date appears to be March 21, 1958, during the boy's state basketball tournament, when the Coliseum opened its doors to Kentucky high schoolers attending the Sweet Sixteen. Quarterfinal games had been played earlier in the day, and the basketball goals remain up for the following day's contests. The signs in the arena promote the evening's celebrity, Len Carl, who worked as a disc jockey at Lexington's radio station WLAP during the late 1950s. The event is interracial despite Lexington's contemporary segregation of many public facilities such as restaurants and buses. A substantial group of Black youth can be seen in the area just to the right of the center of the photo. UK first allowed Black undergraduates to enroll in 1954 following the U.S. Supreme Court decision of Brown vs. Board of Education, which ruled that segregation in public education was unconstitutional. African American graduate and professional students had been permitted to enroll in UK classes beginning in 1949.

Remembering President Kennedy

Top: A memorial service is held in the Coliseum for President John F. Kennedy following his assassination in Dallas in November 1963. The building, first dedicated to the soldiers and sailors who died for their nation, continues to be a place for collective mourning as well as celebration.

Presidential Visits

Right: Presidents, both sitting and former, have spoken to crowds in Memorial Coliseum over several decades. A month before the 1956 presidential election, Dwight D. "Ike" Eisenhower, seeking reelection, made a campaign stop there. Accompanying him was his wife, Mamie, on a stage at the south end of the arena in front of an overflow assembly of supporters seated on the floor and in the stands. In addition to the speech, Eisenhower rode in an open car down Lexington's Main Street, lined ten rows deep with excited onlookers.

Opposite page, top: A more elaborate spectacle occurred when President Lyndon B. Johnson came to the campus on February 22, 1965. He was the keynote speaker at the observance of UK's centennial anniversary held in conjunction with that year's Founders Day convocation. Johnson's speech before a huge assembly of students, faculty, and critics was somewhat disappointing in its brevity and unremarkable content. During his visit, according to UK's president John Oswald, President Johnson seemed in a hurry and irritable. (He may have received negative news concerning the ongoing military fighting in Vietnam during his plane trip to Lexington.) He was presented with the hood of an honorary doctorate, which he reportedly tossed aside offstage as he hastily departed for Washington with his entourage before the larger ceremony had even concluded. Many in the crowd, who had been required to be seated forty-five minutes prior to Johnson's arrival, also rushed for the exits to catch a glimpse of the presidential motorcade heading for the airport at Bluegrass Field.

Bottom: Former President Gerald R. Ford spoke before an audience of 7,000 in April 1977 as part of the John Sherman Cooper Distinguished Lecture Series. He had just recently lost the 1976 presidential election to Jimmy Carter. Ford delivered a speech and then engaged in a question-and-answer session, where he teased that he might run again for the nation's highest office in 1980. However, he never mounted a future presidential campaign.

Intriguing Doorways

Below left: Prior to President Johnson's trip to Lexington in the spring of 1965, the Secret Service had conducted an in-depth security inspection of Memorial Coliseum. President John F. Kennedy had been assassinated in Dallas in November of 1963, and the agency had increased its already highly diligent safety measures. One area of concern for the Secret Service was the lengthy and circuitous route Johnson would have to take between his entry to the Coliseum off the Avenue of Champions and his arrival at the event stage. There was no direct internal path between these points. Instead, the president and his party would have to follow corridors to the northern end of the facility before fully traversing the arena floor in the opposite direction to reach the platform. Deeming this too risky, the Service directed the University to break through a cinder block wall at the end of a passageway for the installation of an extra door. This allowed for a more direct path to the stage through two connected storage spaces. The added door is shown here in 2021. By walking down the steps and then to the right through the visible plywood door, one entered the tall storage alcove that was curtained off from the southern end of the Coliseum floor. The new portal was informally referred to locally as the President Johnson door.

Below right: A fallout shelter sign above a door in an outer corridor of the Coliseum directs people in the direction of, hopefully, safer spaces deep within the arena. This is a Cold War vestige of the 1960s, when the Civil Defense Agency began to identify sturdy public buildings that could protect large numbers of citizens from the radioactive aftermath of a potential nuclear explosion. This assumed that the attack occurred far enough away that there remained survivors who needed cover. The Cold War passed, but the sign remained until at least 2021, when the photo was taken. The President Johnson door is just out of sight to the left at the end of the hallway beyond the door.

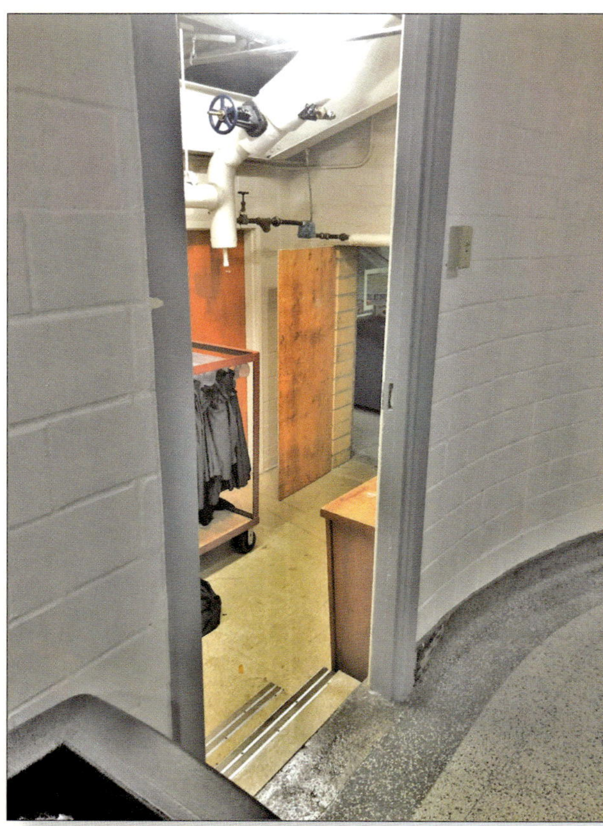

Music for All Tastes

Many famous (at least at the time) pop and rock groups performed in the Coliseum before large crowds of students and townspeople. Some of these events were part of public arts series and others were scheduled by the UK concert committee for students. A sample of musical artists are pictured here, from top left and row by row, with the year that they appeared in the school's Kentuckian yearbook: Louis Armstrong (1960); Brothers Four (1961); Peter, Paul and Mary (1965); The Shirelles (1966); Diana Ross & The Supremes (1969); Chicago (1971).

A Bigger Draw than Basketball

Billy Graham ministers to a crowd at Stoll Field on the first night of his four-day Lexington crusade in April 1971. He would then cross the Avenue of Champions to Memorial Coliseum and preach to the main gathering of the revival. Inside the arena, crowds estimated at 13,500-strong jammed the stands as well as the seating set up on the floor in front of a dais at the south end. A choir of at least a thousand voices had been collected from local churches. Late arrivals were directed each night to the football stadium where loudspeakers relayed the service. The daily combined attendance reached as high as 26,000. The large gatherings resulted in some crusade-goers parking their cars illegally as they sought to be on time. The police did a brisk business in towing cars on the first night, but one officer told a reporter that the drivers remained in good spirits. "They have that real Christian attitude—not like the ball-game crowds," she said. On the second night of the spiritual meeting, Graham addressed the struggles common to young people with a message focusing on—in the vernacular of the day—"hangups."

Professional Tennis in the Coliseum

The above scene is not a mirage. Tennis is really being played in Memorial Coliseum, and at the highest level of competition. The left-handed John McEnroe, pro tennis megastar, serves to Jim Courier, winner of four Grand Slam singles titles. Beginning in the 1990s, longtime UK tennis coach Dennis Emery organized and promoted several professional tennis exhibitions in Lexington to raise significant funds for his tennis program. Two of these events were held in Memorial Coliseum, with a special rubberized mat laid down over the playing floor. The first such match was in December 1991 between Martina Navratilova and Jennifer Capriati. The fifteen-year-old Capriati had defeated the veteran Navratilova in the finals of Wimbledon that summer, and a good crowd was on hand to see the informal rematch. This time Navratilova prevailed in straight sets. However, according to Coach Emery in his book with co-writer John Huang, *Serving Up Winners*, Capriati had inadvertently left her contact lenses at a remote hotel and was visually hampered. In 1994, it was the men's turn when Emery matched the semi-retired John McEnroe with Jim Courier, then the number-three-ranked male player in the world, in the Coliseum. The original opponent for McEnroe was to have been the crowd-pleasing Andre Agassi, but a wrist injury forced him to pull out. About a thousand fans, disappointed with the change to Courier despite his talent, returned their tickets, but the night was still a success as the athletes put on a good show for the still-large turnout.

The UK tennis team had practiced and played matches indoors beginning around 1970 when it acquired an indoor mat. Coach Rupp had congratulated tennis coach Richard Vimont on how he was advancing his program with the indoor setup, but warned him, "If you get a scratch on this court, it's going to be your a--!" Apparently, the tennis players never did damage the Coliseum floor.

Coliseum Craftsmanship

The blueprints for Memorial Coliseum were drawn up immediately after World War II and reflected the Art Moderne form of architecture, which had evolved from Art Deco. The newer style included elements such as rounded corners, geometric shapes, windows constructed of glass blocks, and long horizontal lines. All of these were found inside and outside the Coliseum. Many of these details would be retained in the renovation begun in 2023, but some would not survive. The following images illustrate many of the original, distinctive touches found in the Coliseum prior to its renovation.

Below left: Lexington architect Ernst V. Johnson designed the Coliseum, and his love for fancy brickwork is evident in the upper walls above the lobby entrance. The distinctive M-shaped brick design has been incorporated into the Coliseum's new logo.

Below right: Johnson was a trained brick mason himself, and the local residence he built for his family includes a fireplace featuring the same vertically stacked bricks motif seen here on the Coliseum.

Top: Horizontal and vertical lines of steel, glass, and casing stones frame a distinctive entrance to the shrine for Kentucky's military heroes.

Bottom left: A stout end cap for one of the concrete benches flanking the arena's entry plaza.

Bottom right: Striking grillwork with a "UK" monogram fronts an outside ticket window.

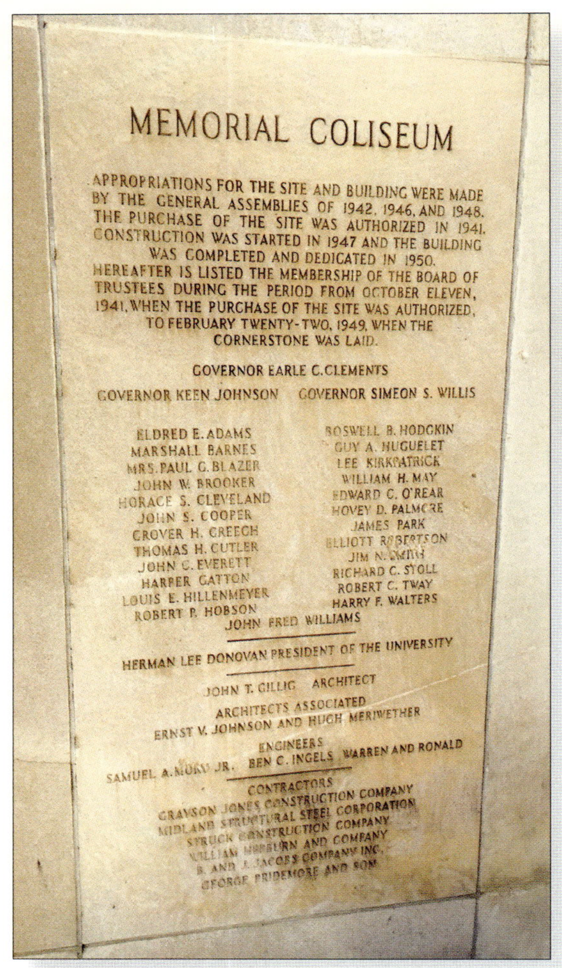

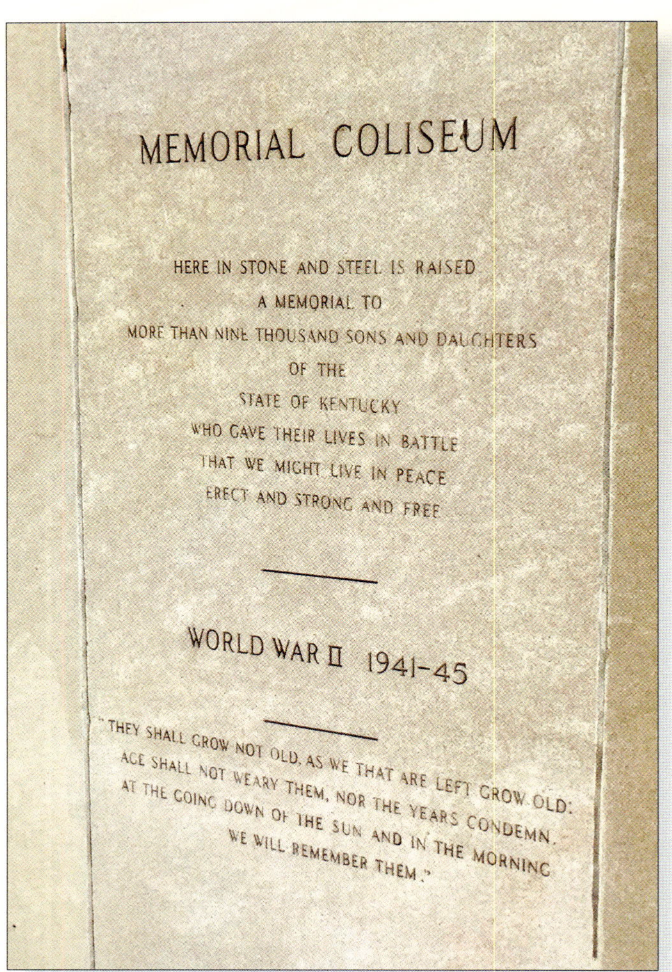

Above left: On either side of the main Coliseum doors are chiseled stone panels. The one to the left of the lobby entrance remembers the architects and public leaders behind its development.

Above right: The panel to the right of the entrance documents the building's purpose:

MEMORIAL COLISEUM

HERE IN STONE AND STEEL IS RAISED
A MEMORIAL TO
MORE THAN NINE THOUSAND SONS AND DAUGHTERS
OF THE
STATE OF KENTUCKY
WHO GAVE THEIR LIVES IN BATTLE
THAT WE MIGHT LIVE IN PEACE
ERECT AND STRONG AND FREE

These words were followed by a quatrain of verse from "The Fallen," by British poet Laurence Binyon:

"THEY SHALL NOT GROW OLD, AS WE THAT ARE LEFT GROW OLD:
AGE SHALL NOT WEARY THEM, NOR THE YEARS CONDEMN.
AT THE GOING DOWN OF THE SUN AND IN THE MORNING
WE WILL REMEMBER THEM."

Top: Opaque windows line the eastern wall of the former swimming pool wing. The round louvered ventilation outlet is expressive of the Art Moderne style. The pool has now been filled in and the space converted to workrooms.

Bottom: Even the most humble fixtures seem to be designed with a sophisticated style. Here, a utility wall outside the pool wing sports geometric fencing.

Top: A gate near the previous utility wall, which matches the fencing's look.

Bottom: Ground level office windows on the west side of the Coliseum are secured by steel grating. This attractive latticework covers the work space once used by Adolph Rupp.

Top: Recessed wall cases lined the pedestrian ramps from the lobby to the concourses. These displayed hand-lettered lists by county of the nearly 10,000 names of Kentuckians killed in World War II.

Center: Fallen service members were further recognized throughout the concourses by approximately 300 bronze stars, each honoring a UK student, faculty, or staff member who was killed in the Second World War. The dates on each star denote the years of their graduation, enrollment, or employment at the University.

Bottom: A small wall plaque in the concourse explained the stars' meaning. The closeup views of the glazed wall tiles reveal that while they appear from a distance to be golden in color, they also are speckled with green.

Top: The outer concourse walls were punctuated with display cases containing UK athletic trophies and pictures. This cabinet exhibits photos of early twentieth century basketball teams.

Bottom: Below the cases are ornamental gratings over ventilation ducts.

Top and bottom: The Coliseum is eye-catching even underfoot. The terrazzo flooring of light and dark brown could still hold a shine many decades after the building's opening.

Bottom: The Art Deco "UK" on the lobby floor is easily overlooked due to its light color, but a treat to discover.

Top and bottom: Stairways in both the concourse and main arena accomplished their function with pleasing forms.

Below: Signage in Memorial was in the striking streamlined style that surely seemed futuristic in 1950. By 2023, it bore a classy vintage look. Kentucky-blue markers guided eventgoers with directions to their seats, Euclid Avenue (now Avenue of Champions), and areas apparently restricted to athletes and UK employees ("Cats").

A Tour of Memorial Coliseum

The following images capture the look and structure of Memorial Coliseum prior to its renovation. They preserve for our memory the original vision of its designers, a foundation that the necessary refurbishments and alterations will partially remove.

A full front view of Memorial Coliseum, such as this one from street level in 2023, was impossible to enjoy for the first twenty-three years of its history. The very close proximity of McLean Stadium, directly across the street on Stoll Field, meant that early photographs of the Coliseum's wide façade had to be taken either from the top of the football stands or at ground level from the side. The Coliseum's designer, Ernst V. Johnson, according to his later architectural partner Byron Ramonowitz, assumed that one day the football field would be demolished and Memorial's grand entrance revealed in full. This occurred in 1974 when McLean Stadium was torn down after the football team moved to the new and much larger Commonwealth Stadium.

Top: Ticket windows, where fans would line up before men's basketball games to hopefully purchase an unclaimed student ticket. These were released to the public five minutes before tip-off.

Bottom: The eastern wing originally housed the University's swimming pool. The squares of brick leaning against the lower wall may be samples for color matching in anticipation of the upcoming renovation.

Top: The southeast corner looking north.
Bottom: The building's east side looking north.

Top: The northeast corner.

Bottom: A panoramic view of the north side of the Coliseum, showing the Joe Craft Center addition.

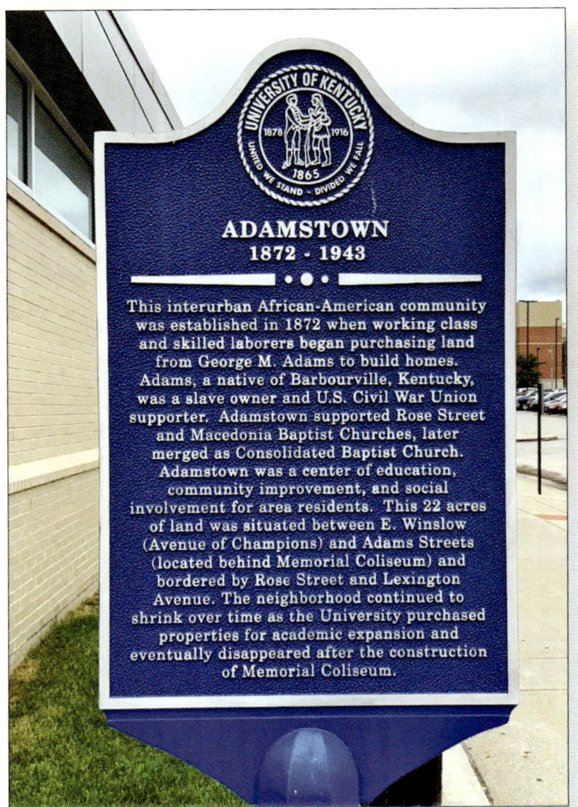

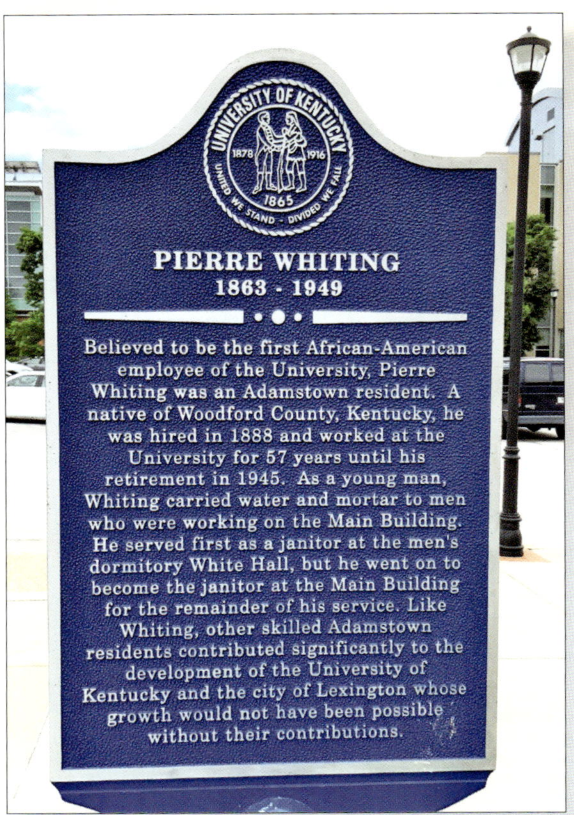

Two sides of the UK historical marker at the Coliseum's northeast corner.

Top left: The face on this panel tells the story of Adamstown, the Black community that once stood on the site and for several blocks beyond.

Top right: The reverse side of the marker details the life of Pierre Whiting, probably the first African American employee of the University of Kentucky and a homeowner within Adamstown.

Bottom: The entrance to the Joe Craft Center on the north side of the Coliseum. Inside are the offices of UK Athletics and practice facilities for men's and women's basketball. Completed in 2007, the addition permanently altered the configuration of the arena space by removing the lower and upper seating of the north "endzone."

Top: A view of the west side of the Coliseum, along Lexington Avenue near the Joe Craft Center addition.

Bottom: Another view of the west side.

Above: The southwest corner. The stair-stepped windows provide ambient light for the pedestrian ramp to the western concourse. Note the small rectangle at the base of the wall marking the cornerstone.

Bottom: A closeup of the cornerstone. The dates encompass the Coliseum's entire planning and construction period.

Top: The horizontal step-backs of the southwest corner capture the varying light and shadows throughout a day.

Bottom: One of the seating areas located on both sides of the Coliseum entrance.

Top: The west ticket windows.

Bottom: To the left of the entry doors is the stone panel chiseled with the names of the architects, engineers, contractors, UK Board of Trustees members, and state leaders involved with the funding and building of the Coliseum.

Top: The main lobby with Adolph Rupp's plaque. The bronze tablet listed Rupp's coaching accomplishments and was presented to him at halftime of a game against Tennessee in January 1975.

Bottom: From the lobby looking east.

Top: A view heading up the west ramp. The wall panels on the right held the list of Kentucky's World War Two dead, while those on the left listed the state's casualties from the Vietnam War. At the top of the walkway, as it bends to the right, were hung framed lists of Kentuckians who sacrificed their lives in the Korean War.

Bottom: Looking back down the west ramp towards the lobby.

Top: Behind the ice locker near the west ramp is a temporary blue wall that hides four original (and forgotten) phone booths, which were recently rediscovered during the Coliseum's renovation. These were probably the booths in which friends of UK players (at least during the Dan Issel-era) were allowed to hide if they did not have game tickets. The players would shepherd the stowaways into the Coliseum through a back door, and once the ticketed crowd started arriving they would emerge from the booths.

Bottom: One-way stairs shuttle fans from the top row of the stands directly down to the concourse, and vice-versa.

Top and bottom: Two views of the west concourse. The author had long been puzzled as to why the cylindrical support columns in these foyers were so large. They appeared to be oversized considering that the enclosed vertical steel beams bolster only the two-story-high concourse wings, and the corresponding pillars in the work-spaces directly below are much smaller. Lexington architect Royce Bourne offered a possible explanation: perhaps the architects purposely designed the broad columns to emphasize the monumental scale of the Coliseum. With this theory in mind, the supports may even be intended to recall the colossal marble columns of ancient Egyptian and Greek temples or mediaeval cathedrals.

Top: Another view of the west concourse.
Bottom: One of the trophy cases in the west concourse.

Top: A vestibule leading to the main arena. Bronze stars on the wall honor UK's World War Two fatalities.

Bottom left: One of the curtained alcoves used as storage space in 1950.

Bottom right: A look fifty feet upwards in 2021 inside the identical alcove across the arena. The alcoves were originally designed to store acoustic panels sliding along overhead steel girders, dividing the Coliseum space into various-sized concert venues. The panels were never installed either due to the cost or the engineering difficulties involved, but the building's acoustics still provided an excellent environment for live music.

Top: Ticket windows (no longer in use) in a west corridor beneath the stands, with the same monogrammed design as those outside the building.

Bottom: A corridor follows the gradual curvature of the seating in the arena above.

Top: A modern view of what was previously the men's varsity basketball locker room.

Bottom left and right: While the wooden lockers and carpeting are recent additions, the blue benches in the left photo may date from the Coliseum's opening. Their appearance is similar to those in a vintage photo on the right of the same room from 1950. In the older image, the mirror on the support column partially reflects a basketball play drawn on the chalkboard of a nearby wall.

Top: Through this gate in the Coliseum's northwest corner, UK Wildcats would move from the nearby locker room onto the playing floor, which is just out of sight to the left. Observers knew that the team was about to emerge when security personnel unlocked the barrier and folded it aside, prompting the arena crowd to explode in cheers of anticipation.

Bottom: Within the corridors on the east side of the Coliseum's ground floor are large storage spaces.

Top: A view from the top of the west stands, looking north to the old balcony. To the left is the windowed control room for sound management and game filming.

Bottom: The upper west stands and control room. These are the original wooden chairs. Row letters are painted on the aisle steps, with each seat number attached to the chairback on a metal tag.

Above: The two seats in the top row on either side of the control room provided only an obstructed view of the court, with the far basket hidden from sight. During at least the Coliseum's early years, these seats were reportedly not ticketed because of this issue. The photo was taken from one of the original impeded-view chairs shortly before the Coliseum was closed for its renovation.

Bottom: Looking at the north balcony from the upper west stands. The balcony became a restricted area well before 2023 (when this photo was taken), and was not open for seating. Below it is an elevated walkway with an entrance to the Joe Craft Center in the middle. The original bleacher seating below the balcony was removed in 1990 to build a complex of athletic rooms, which were later incorporated into the Joe Craft Center.

Top: Looking north along the west stands.

Bottom: A view of the floor from the west stands. The court is set up for a stunt competition. (Stunt is a relatively new sport with teams competing in group acrobatic routines.)

Top: The elevated north walkway looking south. During a press conference in July 2024 to update the public on the state of the renovation, UK Athletic Director Mitch Barnhart revealed that a forgotten room in the ceiling had been rediscovered, complete with a desk. This appears to have been one of two organ chambers, which housed the remote organ pipes for a ground-floor instrument, and hidden by ceiling tiles. Gratings in the compartments' floors for sound propagation also provided a view over the playing floor. In the image here, the organ chambers are located above the two dark rectangles of grating in the middle of the ceiling, just to the right of the hanging speakers.

Bottom: Corner seats in the east bleachers, next to the south wall. Fans sitting here could see the court but not their counterparts in the opposite corner due to the inward angling of the wall.

Top: A look to the north from the southeast corner.
Bottom: The aisle of the east bleachers, looking south.

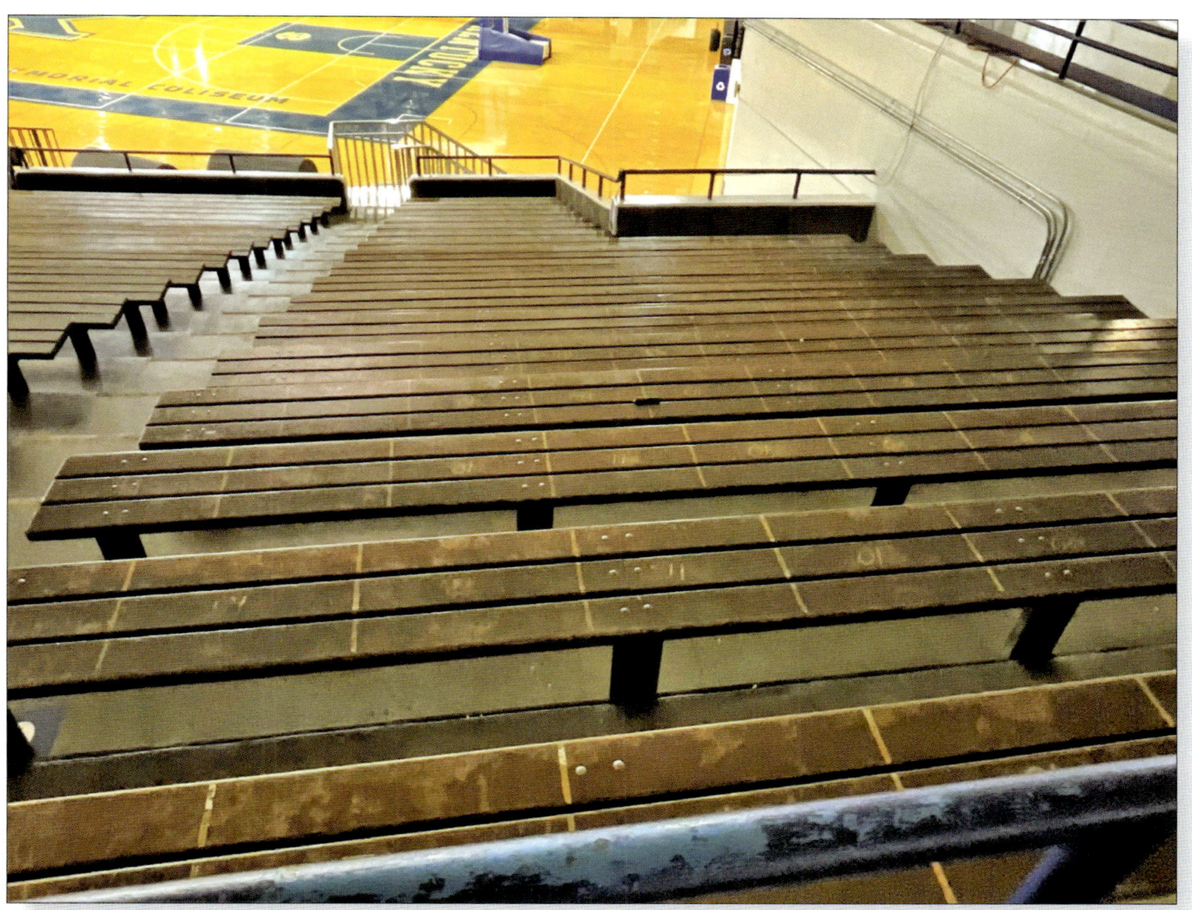

Above: A closeup of the east bleachers. The numbered seating spaces are divided by gold lines. It can be seen that the horizontal ends of the three-deep bleacher boards, along with the bolts attaching them to the steel frames underneath, do not align with the gold lines. The result is an often rough seating experience. The wood from some of these benches was incorporated into the walls of the new south club balcony.

Bottom: Stairs to the secured north balcony.

Above: The old north balcony (now gone), where Wildcat fans once cheered.

Bottom: Looking up at the north balcony. The holes visible in the risers beneath each row of bleachers were part of the Coliseum's ventilation system. Although the arena had no air conditioning until its recent renovation, the holes below every seat in the house were designed to assist in the air circulation throughout the building. The holes were not connected to ductwork but instead opened into storage and workspaces directly below. Apparently, trash and other crowd debris also found its way through the voids and fell into the spaces below.

Above: Looking from the elevated walkway below the Coliseum's north balcony, into the Joe Craft Center.

Bottom: An image from 1950 of the same location as at top, as the Coliseum's first scoreboard is hung on the railing of the north balcony. The two-digit board registered one hundred points as "00." The north concourse (now replaced by the Joe Craft Center) is seen below the scoreboard. Some of the concourse's original brick walls are still visible within the Craft Center's private interior spaces.

Documenting Basketball Success

Three bronze plaques tell the story of Kentucky basketball's winning legacy on the Avenue of Champions.

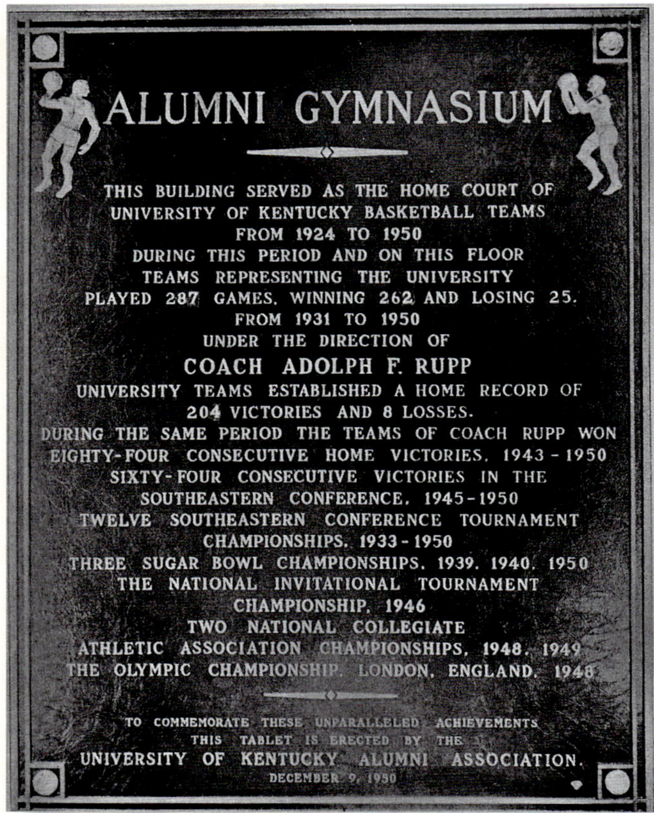

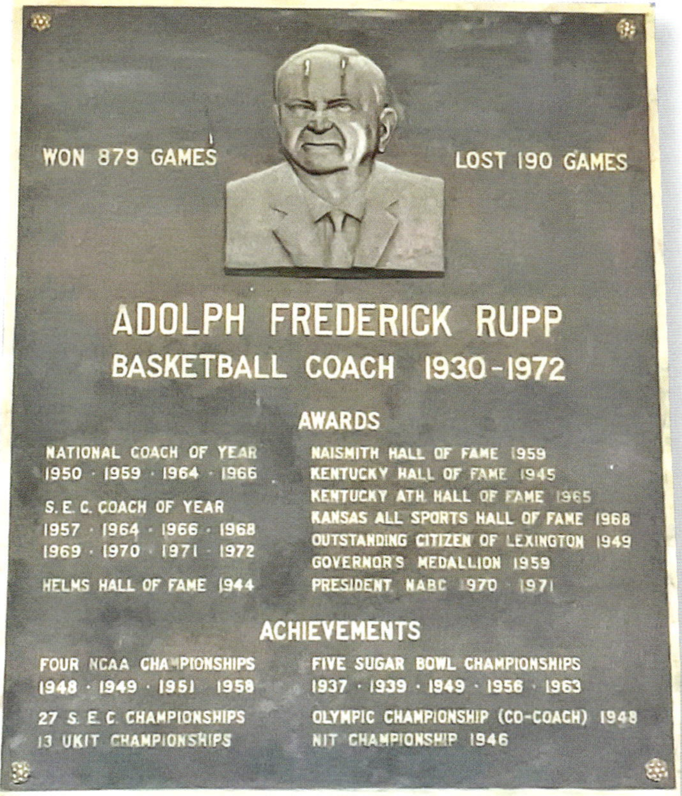

Top left: This tablet was presented by the Alumni Association to document the programs' achievements during its tenure in Alumni Gymnasium. It was attached to the front of the older building in a ceremony on the day of the Wildcats first game in Memorial Coliseum. Today, it hangs at the entrance to the fitness center inside Alumni Gymnasium.

Top right: This large tablet was presented to the retired Adolph Rupp in a halftime ceremony of a game against Tennessee on January 13, 1975. It lists all of the Baron's coaching accomplishments and was mounted inside the Coliseum lobby above the doors leading onto the court.

Bottom: A state historical marker for Coach Rupp standing outside Memorial Coliseum.

The Need for Renovation

Showing Its Age

Top and bottom: After seventy-plus years, Memorial Coliseum's bones remained solid but its finish was fading and, in some places, crumbling. Plaster peeled from the roof and walls of the lobby, lower pedestrian ramps, and concourse stairwells. The images here are from just before the renovation began.

Damage Big and Small

Top: The World War Two honor roll panels are slightly faded from decades of sunlight exposure through the ramp windows, and some have sustained water damage.

Bottom left: Caulking repairs mar the southern arena wall.

Bottom right: Wear and tear to the building extends to its exterior, where the roof edgings above the ticket windows are significantly deteriorated. All of these images of structural damage were taken just prior to the major Coliseum renovation begun in the summer of 2023.

RENOVATING THE COLISEUM

After nearly 75 years, the grand structure of Memorial Coliseum was coming apart at the seams, with amenities that were far outdated. Although large ceiling fans had been added to the arena decades ago, there had never been air conditioning in the facility beyond the Joe Craft Center addition, and there were peeling plaster walls and ceilings for all to see. Over the years, the scoreboard and lighting had been modernized, but the seats (all original wood) were uncomfortable and the framed panels honoring Kentucky's war fatalities were fading. Even the pedestrian ramps up to the concourses were regarded by modern crowds as quite steep.

To preserve Memorial for years to come while remaking its interior into a cutting-edge facility for a new era, the University hired RossTarrant Architects of Lexington as designers, and Congleton-Hacker, a regional construction firm with Lexington origins, as general contractors. The renovation was budgeted for eighty-two million dollars and scheduled to take approximately eighteen months. While the extensive work was carried out, the athletic offices inside the adjacent Craft Center remained occupied, but the women's basketball, gymnastics, volleyball, and stunt programs had to host their home matches elsewhere. Most of their competitions were held at Rupp Arena, with some moved to Transylvania University's Clive M. Beck Center. All but women's basketball also had to practice elsewhere. (Women's basketball retained access to their own practice court within the Joe Craft Center.)

By the fall of 2024, the outside of the Coliseum was still very much a work site, while the arena's interior was largely finished. It was clear that the old building would have an impressive new future. Athletic events returned in the fall of 2024, with each varsity sport individually celebrating its homecoming to the arena. A formal and full reopening ceremony for Memorial Coliseum was planned for the spring of 2025.

December 2023

Bottom: Work began in the spring of 2023. Here, the Coliseum's entire outside entry court has been removed, including cement benches and landscape beds. The photograph was taken on December 20, 2023.

Early Spring 2024

Top: By March 2024, the arena's interior transformation was well under way. This view is from the Joe Craft Center's entrance on the arena's raised north walkway. The ceiling beams are exposed, the basketball court has been taken up, and the seats have been removed. At the far end of the arena above the lobby doors, a new balcony for a luxury club seating area has been framed with steel. To make room for this addition and its access, a section of the stands (the concrete tiers on which the individual seats will be bolted) abutting the bare end walls to the left and right of the lobby have been removed.

Bottom: A photo from the same day as the one above, with a view shifted slightly to the right. In the center-right of the image, a section of the wall along the walkway at the top of the lower stands has been removed. This serves to significantly enlarge the vomitorium (or public accessway) between the concourse and the arena seating. The same modification was also done to the opposite side of the Coliseum.

Late Spring 2024

Top: In May 2024, the front entrance has been extended forward by enclosing the formerly open portico with glass windows and moving the original entry doors.

Bottom: By May 2024, the new colorful ceiling was far along. Also, the steel framework for the luxury balcony accommodations at the far south end had been solidified in concrete. The back of this new seating area would open out above the front lobby vestibule. The new wooden flooring is being laid down in strips, while a video scoreboard is being framed to hang from the central ceiling.

Late Spring 2024

Top: Along the Avenue of Champions beside the arena, the construction safety fence is covered with some of the architectural renderings revealing the future look of the finished renovation.

Summer 2024

Bottom: The new playing floor and blue bleachers for the east stands (on the left) have been fully installed in early August 2024. Large rotating fans hang above the seating and will combine with a new AC system to banish the old days of a sweltering Coliseum. The west stands still lack their chair-style seats. The four-sided video board has been lowered from the ceiling, with its screen in test mode. The balcony club area at the far end nears its final form. The court will be ready in a few weeks for a volleyball exhibition match between Kentucky and Dayton that will be closed to the public. The first official athletic event for the renovated Coliseum was scheduled for August 30, when UK volleyball would take on Northern Kentucky.

The Architects' Vision

The following images by RossTarrant Architects are courtesy of UK Athletics, showing what the interior of Memorial Coliseum would look like when the renovation was complete.

Top: A view of the arena from the northeast corner.

Bottom: The renovated Coliseum lobby. At above left, the back of the new club mezzanine opens onto this area. The hanging lists of Kentucky war fatalities have been replaced by monitors replicating the rolls of honor. The pedestrian access on the right to the east concourse now has steps instead of a ramp. The Art Deco-style UK monogram remains on the entry floor.

Top: One of the refurbished concourses.

Bottom: The plush new club (looking westward) runs the length of the south end of the Coliseum. It incorporates the old fifty-foot-tall storage alcoves that flanked the court. The open back end offers views through the lobby windows onto the Avenue of Champions and the UK campus. Part of its walls incorporate wood from the original bleacher seating.

Memorial Coliseum in all its glory, following its reopening for varsity volleyball on August 30, 2024.

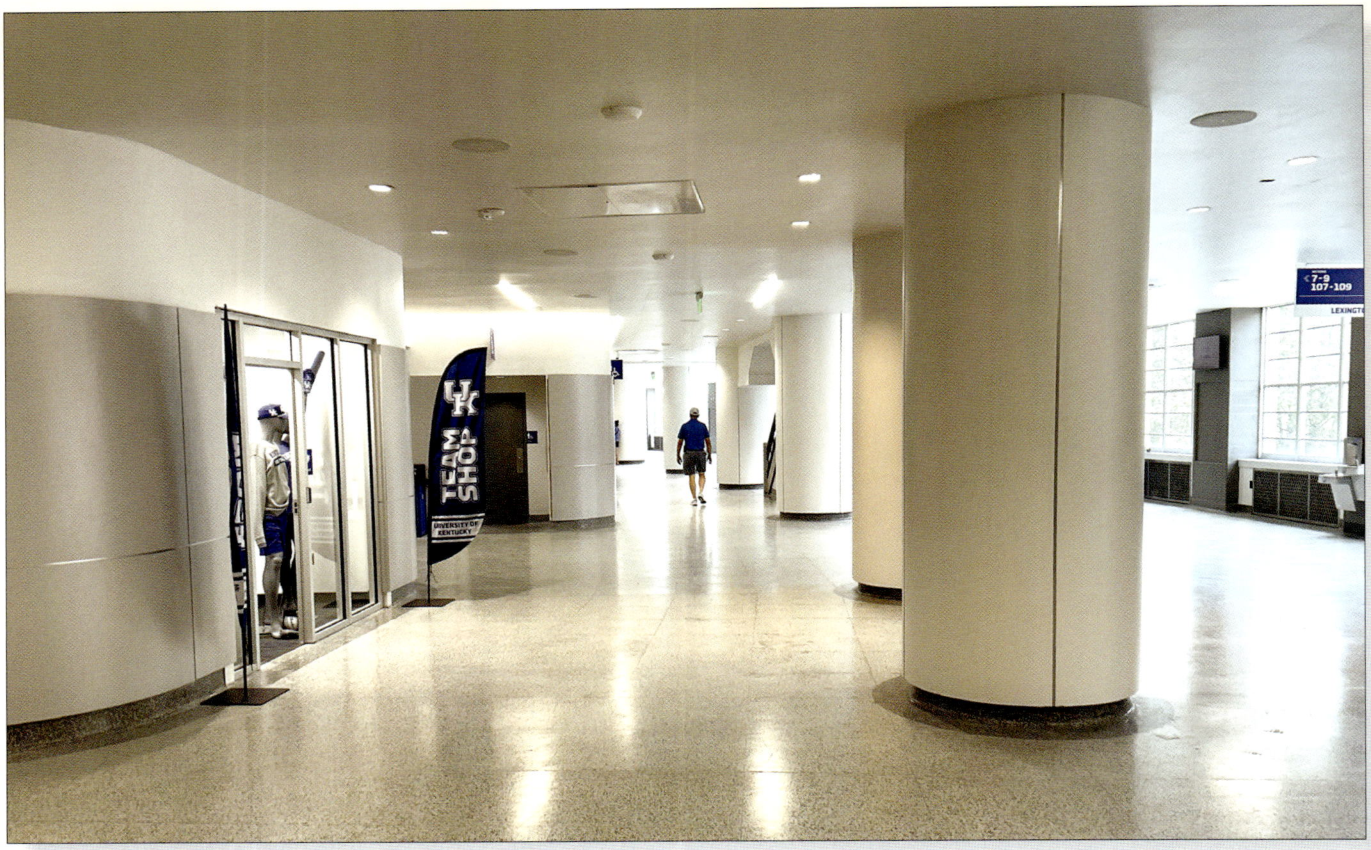
UK
TEAM SHOP
UNIVERSITY OF KENTUCKY
7-9
107-109

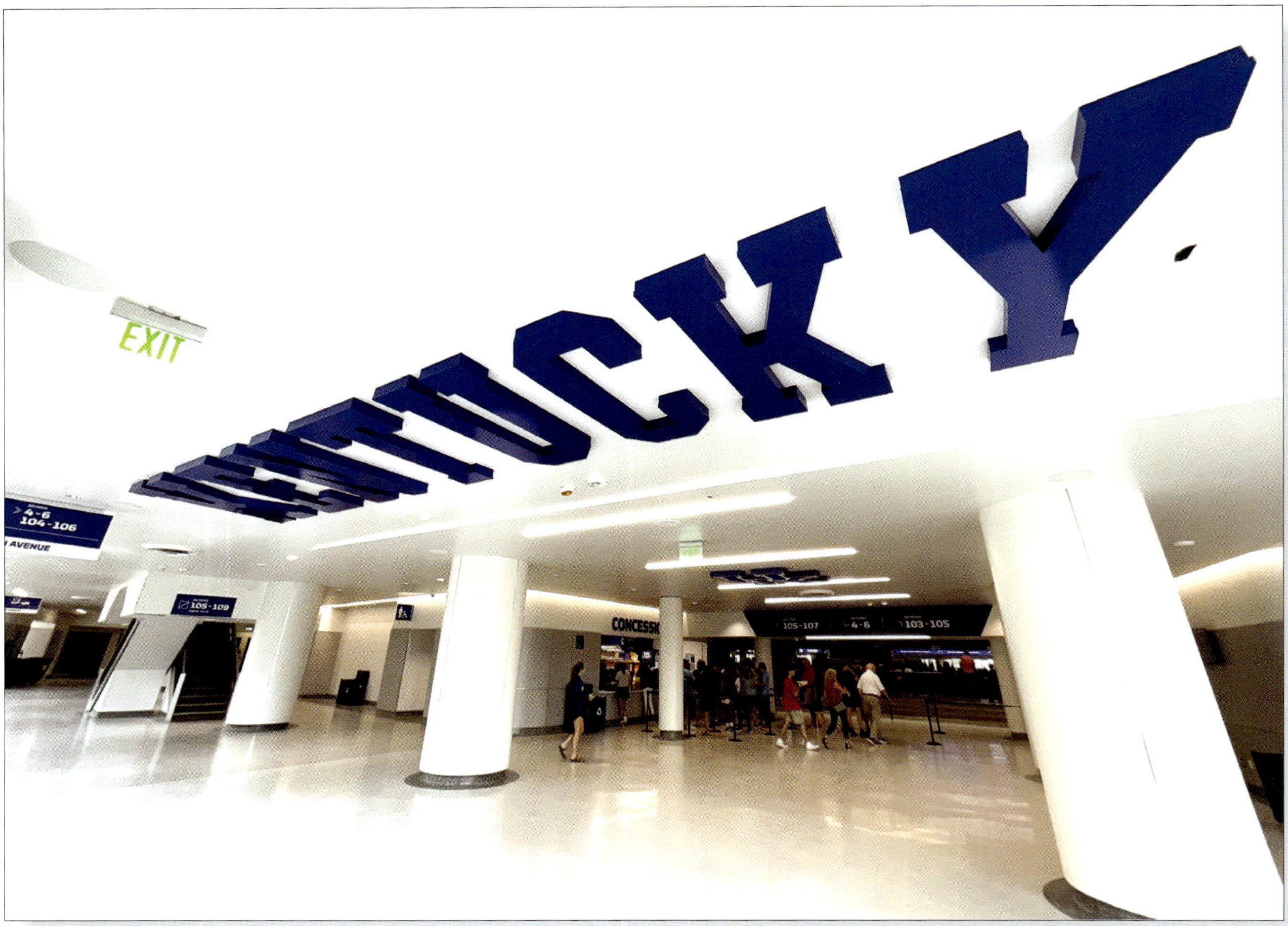
EXIT
4-6
104-106
105-109
105-107
4-6
103-105

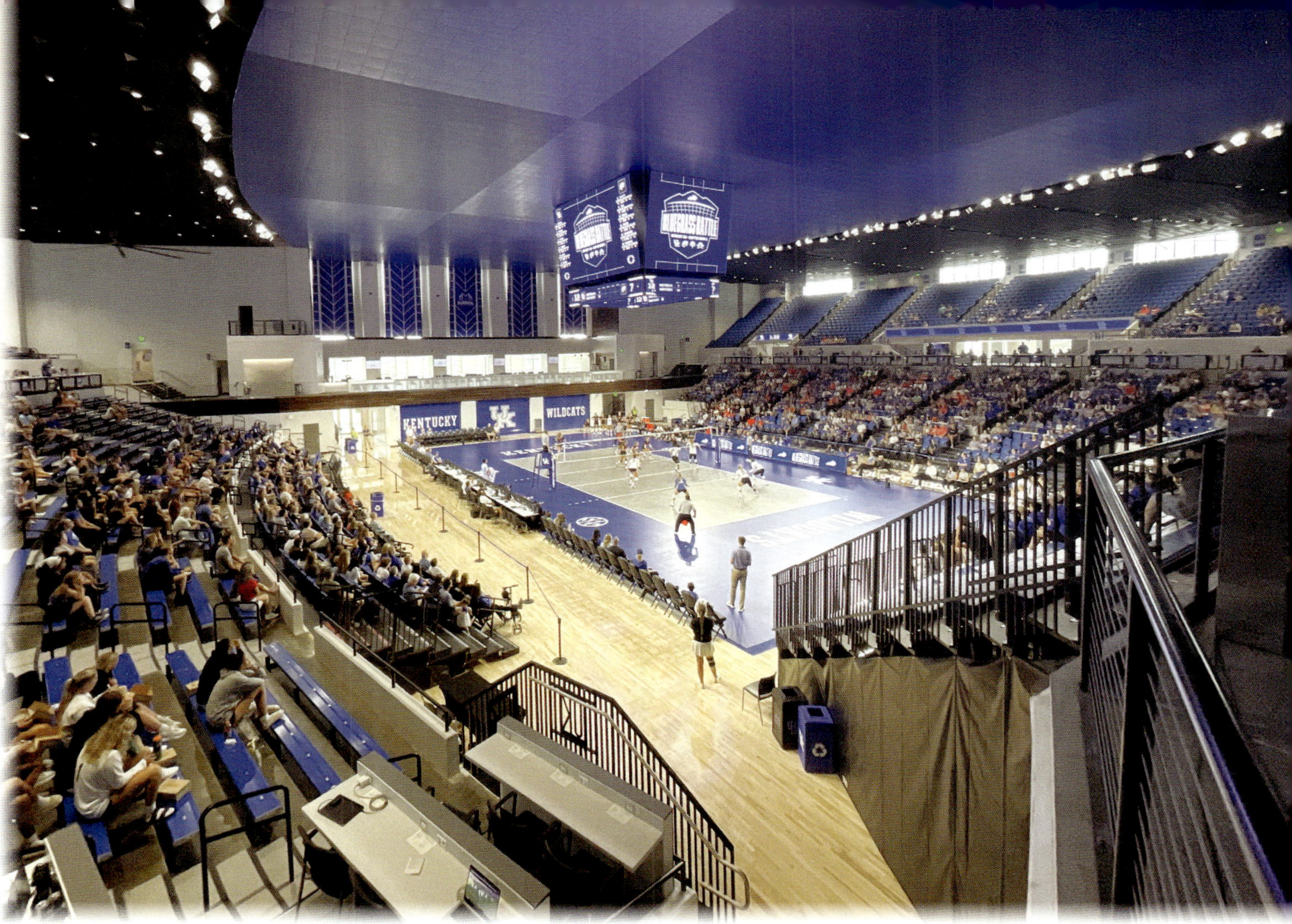
KENTUCKY
WILDCATS

KENTUCKY
TODAY'S MATCH UP

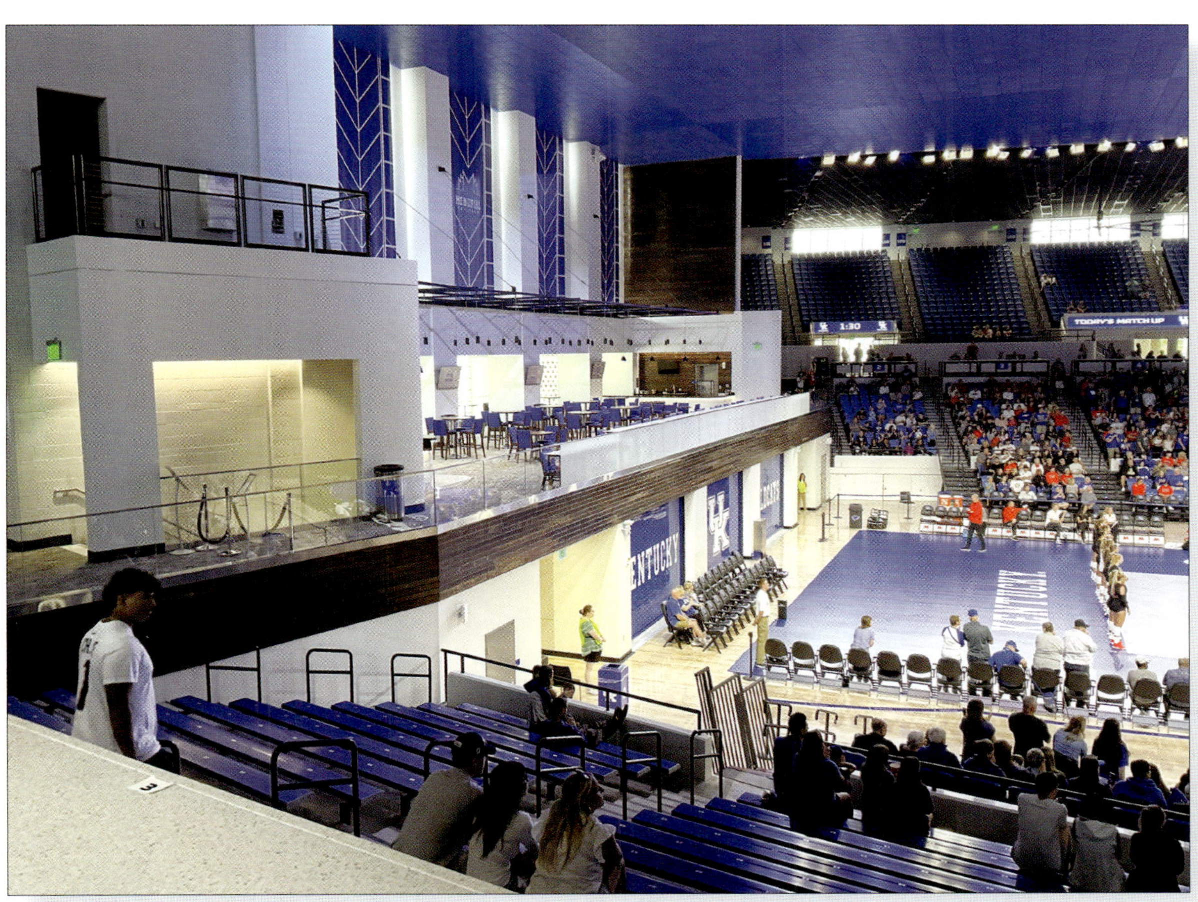

Photo by Bob Willcutt.

Memories of the Coliseum

Nearly everyone who has stepped inside Memorial Coliseum over the years has strong and fond memories of the impressive building. The following are personal memories from those who performed, worked, and watched inside its walls.

Todd Cook

Asbury College (now University) graduate, author, and Wilmore, Kentucky, resident

My first memories of Memorial Coliseum are from the 1974-75 basketball season. At the time our family had been in Kentucky for less than a year, but we were already fans of the Kentucky Wildcats and the ABA Kentucky Colonels. While we were able to follow the Wildcats more on TV, our first in-person game at Memorial Coliseum was to see the Kentucky Colonels play the Utah Stars. It was March of 1975. The Colonels featured larger-than-life stars like Dan Issel, Louie Dampier, and Artis Gilmore. They would take on a Stars' squad featuring recent high school phenom Moses Malone. We arrived early, so as we stood outside waiting for the gates to open, my brother Scott was able to open the door to the main lobby for the arriving Utah Stars, decked out in their early '70s urban finery (long leather or fur-lined coats, tilted hats, sunglasses). Once inside, I recall marveling at the high flat (not domed) Coliseum ceiling I had seen so many times on TV. My brothers and I took a pre-game walk up to the old bleachers overlooking the far end of the court. I couldn't believe how OLD the bleachers looked, how high up they were, and how STEEP they were. My impressions of the game were as follows: Artis Gilmore intimidating a young, skinny Malone into wild hook shots; Dan Issel looking like a massive mountain of a man as he thundered down court; Bird Averitt coming off the bench to take every shot — and make nearly every one — in garbage time.

Dan Issel

UK basketball All-American, UK men's basketball's all-time leading scorer, and Naismith Memorial Hall of Fame member

When the Coliseum was built, many people thought it would be a "white elephant" and never be filled. But the crowds were so large for our games that it was hard to get into the Coliseum. I recall how intimate it was with the large crowds and that many couldn't get in.

I also recall how stark the locker room was. We sat on wooden benches that were bolted to the floor and the lockers were the old steel type. Today's players would not be impressed. It was the same situation in the meeting room underneath the stands across from the old ticket windows. We had team meetings there where we watched game film with the coaches, which was something fairly new at the time. There were just plain benches in that room, too, and no fancy extras.

Some of the players would help out friends who didn't have a game ticket by letting them sneak into the Coliseum early through a locked side door. The friends would then hide in the concourse pay phone booths until the arena was opened for the game. This was usually done after the team's pregame meal in the student center, when some of the players would come to the Coliseum for a pregame nap on bunkbeds which were near the locker room. Once, Mike Pratt went to let in a friend while Mike Casey served as lookout and sat on the floor around the corner. Coach Rupp unexpectedly appeared in the hallway and asked Casey what he was doing. In order to distract Rupp from seeing what Pratt was up to nearby, Casey said that he wasn't feeling well. He "recovered" enough to have a great game that night, and afterwards on the postgame radio show Coach Rupp raved about him to Cawood Ledford: "That Casey was sick tonight, but he played through it and had a tremendous game!"

Ralph Hacker

Longtime color and play-by-play broadcaster for UK men's basketball and football, as well as high school sports; member of multiple halls of fame including the UK Athletics Hall of Fame

The first time I saw a basketball game in Memorial Coliseum was around 1959. The teams I do not remember, but it was the KHSAA Boys tournament and the excitement was unreal. Along with my teammate from Madison Central High School, arrangements had been made by our coach, Russell "Buddy" Roberts, to purchase tickets for one day. We left Richmond early that morning to witness the first of six games. With the exception of leaving between games 4-6, when we walked to downtown Lexington to look around, we were in the building all day long, coming back for games 5 & 6. That means it was Thursday, for at that time there were two games on Wednesday night, six on Thursday, four on Friday, and two on Saturday including a consolation game.

I didn't realize that in 1966 I would be broadcasting both high school and UK freshmen games, later joining the University of Kentucky Basketball Radio Network and being a part of that team until 2002. Included in that schedule was the final game the men's basketball Wildcats played in this Mecca of College Basketball.

What a thrill to see all the great players and great teams who graced that floor, to get to know the players who would become legendary, and the coaches who already were. To work alongside the great Voice of The Wildcats, Cawood Ledford. Working beside Cawood was always a thrill; he never held back. Like the night Kentucky was playing someone and according to Cawood an absolutely horrendous call was made by the official. It happened at the opposite end of the floor from our broadcast spot. After ranting for a moment or two he turned to me and said, "What do you think about that call, Ralph?" I replied, "I don't know Cawood, it was too far away for me to see." He then replied, "'Ralph the Lion Hearted,' 18 years younger than me with 20-20 vision and no guts." Perhaps that is the moment I began saying, "That's right, Cawood."

I became a UK fan from listening to games Claude Sullivan broadcast from Memorial Coliseum, and have remained one forever.

After finishing broadcasting freshmen games, I would go to the endzone of the Coliseum and sit in one of the assigned seats to watch the varsity play. As a rule, my seatmate was Oscar Combs, then of the *Hazard Herald*. One particular night, I believe it was Ronnie Lyons throwing the ball inbounds. He proceeded to throw a pass from out of bounds in front of us to, I believe, Jim Andrews. Instead, he overthrew his man and the ball went through the net ninety-four feet away. Longest made basket I ever saw. Didn't count, you can't make a basket from out of bounds.

When broadcasting a UKIT game for, as I recall, Iowa, who did not send a broadcast team for the game, I felt a presence of someone sliding into the empty seat beside me. During the next commercial break, the man asked if I needed a color man. I, of course, said yes. That color man was Adolph Rupp, on his way to becoming the winningest basketball coach of all times. I was back broadcasting the championship game the next night, while Coach was back on the bench.

I saw Dale Brown of LSU as a young coach throw his coat on the floor and stomp it saying, "Take my coat, you have taken the game!" Saw Mike Pratt in a game against Dayton take an elbow to the nose, moving it to the side of his face. He grabbed it, snapped it back into place, and continued to play.

Those were the times, my friends, we all hoped they would never end.

The players and coaches of Memorial Coliseum were of a special and rare breed. The fans were so special that visiting teams feared entering the door. As a gentle lady said to Cawood one night as we were leaving the gym, "Cawood, I liked it better when we would just kill the other team." He replied, "We beat them by twenty-five." She said, "It should not have been that close."

There are so many stories, so many people, so many games. All together they make Memorial Coliseum, or perhaps Memorial makes them.

We all remember that final game in 1972 when the house lights went down, something the lighting director Dick Dickson did not like to do because the lighting system at that time was temperamental. A spotlight opened on to the north corner of the floor, and with hands raised Adolph F. Rupp walked onto the Coliseum floor as Head Coach for the final time.

Alan Sullivan

Son of legendary UK sports radio announcer Claude Sullivan, architect, and author of a biography of Claude's life

In 1950, Claude Sullivan broadcast the first game at Memorial, and continued through the 1966 Rupp's Runts' NCAA runner-up season. I was born in 1951 and started going to the games with my mother in 1958, alternating with my older brother, David. From 1960 to 1967 we helped produce the games for Sullivan Enterprises on the Standard Oil Sports Network. Our midcourt press table seats and two spectator seats three rows behind were across the aisle from Happy Chandler and William Shatner — a unique vantage point.

Claude announced his 1951 Clark County high school team to the first state high school tournament championship held in Memorial Coliseum, and in 1953 the first UKIT holiday tournament that included Duke, LaSalle, and a UCLA team coached by John Wooden. I later witnessed Bill Bradley of Princeton and Jerry West of West Virginia play in the UKIT. In 1955 Claude announced Georgia Tech's 59-58 defeat of UK that snapped their 129-game home winning streak. In 1958 Claude made the famous call of the triple overtime game with Vernon Hatton's game-tying midcourt shot against Temple.

My greatest thrill in Memorial Coliseum was attending every Rupp's Runts game from the midcourt press table working as statistician with Claude. After each broadcast my job took me to the UK locker room to escort Adolph back to my seat for his post-game interview with Claude. This was the most exciting team I ever witnessed. I was one of the few that were able to see the Rupp's Runts team practice in Memorial with Claude.

I fondly recall how loud the crowd could be at Memorial, especially the games with Alabama and Coach C. M. Newton where Adolph put up one hundred-plus points. The fans stomped on the metal grating of the first rows of temporary seating, making reverberations off the hard concrete block walls so loud that you couldn't talk — a sound that was never reproduced in Rupp Area.

Rex Payne

Member of the Committee of 101 for nearly sixty years

The Committee of 101 was established in 1966, and the first year we started working in Memorial Coliseum as ushers was 1967. I joined the 101 at that time and we then had 166 members, mostly as ushers. Our first sport coats were dark blue, which we got from Graves Cox clothiers, with grey pants. I had also worked as a Boy Scout usher in the early '50s at the state tournaments in the Coliseum. Memorial Coliseum is a very special place, and every time I walked into it I got a feeling of awe, wonder and pride. I still do.

Larry Vaught

Veteran UK sports reporter and commentator in print, online, and on radio

Memorial Coliseum is such an iconic place. I grew up listening to UK basketball games being played in Memorial Coliseum on the radio. As a UK student from 1970-74, I got to attend games and watch legendary coach Adolph Rupp in his final years. I saw Jimmy Dan Conner, Kevin Grevey, and Mike Flynn play freshmen games. I loved as a student lining up outside the Coliseum and then running to claim the best seat possible when the doors opened. It was a dynamic setting for basketball with so many seats so close to the floor. It was also a history lesson for a youngster like myself to just be in the same place where so many legendary players worked their magic.

Jim Andrews

UK basketball star and First Team All-SEC center

My first introduction to Memorial Coliseum was in the 1968-69 season on my official visit to Kentucky. It may have been one of the last recruiting introductions, as the practice was deemed too much of a recruiting advantage. I must admit it had a big influence on my decision to come to Kentucky. What was to follow was only the beginning of many memorable moments capped by tremendous games against SEC opponents. The two most memorable were the Alabama game where we jumped to a 22-0 lead, and all of the Tennessee games capped by the hail of oranges after the unicyclist attempted a layup during warmups, and then surpassed by my winning basket against Tennessee in Coach Rupp's final season which helped inspire "The Huddle" [an artist's print] currently in the Naismith Hall of Fame. Memorial Coliseum was not only where we practiced and played games but it housed a number of events, including registration and drop-add for classes, but also some of the greatest concerts I ever attended, including The 5th Dimension, Bill Withers, and Chicago. More importantly, during my conditioning and running along the concourse, I was able to understand that the true purpose of this building was the honor of the starred plaques with the names of those who gave the ultimate sacrifice to protect our freedoms.

Mike Murphy

Team manager for UK men's basketball from 1976 to 1980, including the 1978 NCAA championship team

As a young kid growing up in Lexington, Memorial Coliseum was a revered place. When I was ten years old, I began selling Cokes at the Coliseum during all basketball games. The UK band sat right at half-court in those days, and they took me under their wing and bought all their Cokes from me. They also invited me to sit with them for the last ten minutes of the games. My fondest memories were getting to watch some of the all-time great UK Players — Dan Issel, Mike Pratt, Pat Riley, Tom Parker, to name only a few — but also the great SEC players of the day, highlighted by the likes of "Pistol" Pete Maravich, Bernard King, and Ernie Grunfeld. One of my cool memories from being a manager was the first day of practice on the court at the Coliseum my freshman year, and the smell of burning rubber from the Converse shoes we wore in those days during the drills that Joe B had the team run. I had been around hoops forever but had never, ever encountered something like that.

Buddy Rosenberger

Member of the Committee of 101 for nearly fifty years

In my younger days I helped park cars for basketball games in the bowling alley parking lot beside the Coliseum with Gary Barlow. I was on my trial year with the Committee before I was actually active in the 101, which was the last year of playing in Memorial. The next year I became active and worked with John Walters in Rupp. I attended UK from 1957 to 1961 and attended every game during that time in Memorial on my student ID card.

Tom Leach

Voice of the Wildcats for men's basketball and football

A good friend of my father was in a position to control the season tickets for UK games for a company for which he worked, and he would invite my dad and me to a few Wildcat games each season. What a treat that was for a young UK basketball fan. It felt like the building shook when the Cats were running down the ramp onto the court for pregame warmups, and the game I remember most was one against Tennessee. Ray Mears' teams were UK's biggest challengers for the SEC title in those days when only the league champ made the NCAA Tournament. Mears was a brash challenger to the Rupp-coached Kentucky teams, in the role that Dale Brown and others would later play against Joe B. Hall. Mears had a player who rode a unicycle during the pregame layup line. I vividly remember Mears standing next to SEC broadcaster Joe Dean for an interview, and when the camera's red light was illuminated the UK students stood up and pelted Mears with orange slices. I regret that I never had the chance to watch one of the matchups between Kentucky and "Pistol" Pete Maravich's LSU teams, but any chance to watch the Cats play at Memorial Coliseum was one of my highlights for the year.

Kevin Cook

Author

In March of 1975, the Kentucky Wildcats had beaten the previously undefeated Indiana Hoosiers in an NCAA Regional final to reach the Final Four. This was my first year of rooting for UK and the tenacious victory had me euphoric. During the ensuing week before Kentucky traveled on to San Diego for the NCAA semifinals, my parents took me and my brothers to watch the Kentucky Colonels play the Utah Stars in an ABA matchup in the Coliseum, my first time in that building. We had lower-level seats in the east stands, and the most memorable feature of the arena for me were the large championship banners hung on the tall end wall above the lobby doors.

Prior to the ABA contest, two youth teams competed in an exhibition while some of the pros came out of the dressing rooms and sat courtside to watch. I and other kids in the crowd grabbed pen and paper, then headed for the athletes to gather autographs. From the Colonels, I collected the signature of future hall-of-famer Artis Gilmore. Then I spied rookie Moses Malone of the Utah Stars, a teenage phenom and one of the first players to jump directly from high school to the professional ranks. I handed him a small piece of scrap paper that my mom had scrounged from her purse, and he dutifully signed it. Then he paused, turned the paper over, and signed it again!

Karen Marlowe

UK Athletics staff, and daughter of beloved former UK men's basketball equipment manager Bill "Mr. Wildcat" Keightley

All of my memories in Memorial blend into one big happy one with Daddy. There are not a lot of specific events, but bits and pieces of many. As a young child I remember going to some games there. Dad was not on the bench then, so he sat with us. My cousins, the Fallises, sat next to us, and Ann, who was three years younger than me, and I would go down on the sidelines at halftime and pick up the paper strings from the cheerleaders' pom-poms. That was a treat for us; we would shake our little fistfuls of string just like they were the real thing.

I also remember going to "The Cage," which was the equipment room before the wall was put on the front of it. It was heavy diamond wire, and everything inside was completely visible. During Dad's time, a wall was constructed after the wire was cut one night. They called him to tell him what happened. Even though the Coliseum was being watched by UK Police, he got his rifle and sat in the cage the rest of the night. No one said a word to him about doing so!

As a student, I spent more time with him in the equipment room between classes. I got to know the players and managers that were my age then, and as a result feel the closest connection to them. It was always a wonderful time spent with him there, you never knew who would walk in or what adventure would happen for that day! I treasure every second of that time in my life and would like nothing more than to return to it.

Before the construction began on the remodel, I took the nameplate off of the wall, not knowing if his room would remain. Thankfully, it will, and so I will put the plaque back in its proper place when the construction is finished. It needs to remain there always!

Jack Pattie

Local fixture of the Central Kentucky community for decades as radio host of "Lexington Morning News with Jack Pattie" on WVLK

My first memory of Memorial Coliseum was attending a concert there with a friend around 1963. I would have been about 11 years old. It was a Peter, Paul and Mary concert and I brought along a copy of their *Moving* album in hopes of obtaining autographs from the group. I remember being awed by the enormity of the Coliseum. I had never seen anything like it. It was a wonderful concert and at the end, my friend and I headed for the door to meet Peter, Paul and Mary, but they weren't there. So, we boldly began running through the halls (remember, we were goofy eleven-year-olds), until we came to a room with an open door and there standing before us was Peter Yarrow and Paul Stookey! They kindly signed my album and Peter even did a small caricature of himself. We never found Mary, but I was so thrilled to get autographs from the other two, it didn't even matter. The record has long gone missing, but I still, and will always, have my album cover and wonderful memories of Memorial Coliseum.

Eric Lindsey

Formerly Director of Communications and Public Relations for UK Men's Basketball

I would imagine most people's fondest memories of Memorial Coliseum lie somewhere in the ninety-four feet of hardwood at the center of the arena, or from the friendly confines of the classic wooden bleachers and seats. And, undoubtedly, some of the very best, obviously, occurred there. But for me, given my former role as the director of communications and public relations for men's basketball, my fondest memories reside in the media room. Although most of the recent men's basketball press conferences were moved to the Joe Craft Center under John Calipari, the Memorial Coliseum media room was still utilized for the larger media gatherings, like media day.

Although I witnessed the media day spectacle year after year, it always amazed me when we would weave through the back hallways in the underbelly of Memorial, swing through the door and into the media room for the big event. Staring at you were more than one hundred people in a room that couldn't have been bigger than 1,500 square feet, crammed with reporters (of course), photographers, and UK Athletics staffers. Obviously, they weren't there to see me — I was just a part of organizing the day — but to walk out each time and see the rows of cameras and eyes on the head basketball coach was an annual reminder to me how much this place cares for its hoops. I never took for granted the people who sat in that seat behind that microphone annually — Calipari, Tubby Smith, Rick Pitino, Joe B. Hall, and even Adolph Rupp – to set the stage for the upcoming season.

Sure, it was just a media session, but media day was as much for the fans as it was for the outlets in the room. It was a chance to set the tone for the upcoming season. In more recent times, Big Blue Madness has become the unofficial marker of the basketball season, but for me, it was always media day.

Dick Parsons

UK basketball guard, All-American shortstop for UK baseball, head coach of Wildcat baseball, assistant basketball coach for Adolph Rupp and Joe B. Hall, member of the UK Athletics Hall of Fame

We were playing Tulane about 1960 in the Coliseum, when the UK bench was located under the goal. We scored three early baskets, then Tulane's center, Jack Arden, scored three baskets in return. When he scored, Coach Rupp would jump out of his seat and yell, "He's Walking!" It happened again and Rupp yelled, "That man is walking!" The score was six to six and Rupp called time out. He told me to go get George Conley, one of the referees. [George Conley was the father of Larry Conley, later a star player on Rupp's Runts.] George was also a Kentucky state senator from Ashland. When I told Conley that Rupp wanted to see him, he asked why, but I told him that I didn't know. When Rupp saw Conley walking over to the bench he said in his drawl, "Sen-a-tor, if I'm not mistaken, you have proposed a twenty-million-dollar road bill for your district. But I don't think you will need it." "*Why not?*" Conley asked. "Because," Rupp answered, "you can just have everybody in Ashland walk everywhere they go." Coach Rupp wanted to avoid getting technical fouls, so he often used a humorous approach to make his point. On the next Tulane play, Conley called a walking violation and had a kind of embarrassed smile on his face.

Dr. Jack Ditty

UK varsity tennis player, member of the Kentucky Tennis Hall of Fame, doctor of dermatology

When we were students at UK during the years of 1967 to 1971, my wife, Juanita, and I were excited to go watch the Wildcats play basketball at Memorial Coliseum. The most exciting game of the year was when UK played LSU with Pete Maravich. Pete Maravich was the most outstanding college basketball player at that time. He was an exciting player to watch and there would be a big crowd. There would be more students wanting to get in the game than they had room. We didn't actually get tickets. They just allowed the students to come in with the student ID. That night when Pete Maravich was playing, there were so many people that there were around one hundred students extra. One of the administrators made an announcement to all the people waiting to get in that if we would just be patient and wait at the door to the floor of the Coliseum, they would have an announcement for us. He came back in a few minutes and said, "All right, nobody say a word. We want you to walk onto the floor and sit down next to the sideline, and just be quiet and don't say anything." So we all sat around the floor of the basketball court. We got to watch Pete Maravich play against the Wildcats with that view from the floor. During the game a loose ball bounced towards me and I caught it, and then Pete Maravich was standing there and I passed it back to him. It was the thrill of a lifetime during my four years at UK that night.

I had many experiences besides that at the Coliseum because UK tennis team coach Dick Vimont trained us by running around the concourse. That was one of the main parts of our training, and then after we did our running we would go to the boiler room and lift weights. He wanted us to train in the heat like we would be exposed to in Florida when we played our first spring matches there. UK's basketball team practiced until about 9 o'clock, so we were going in for our training with our running and weightlifting while the UK basketball team was still practicing. Coach Rupp did not allow anyone to watch practice, so there was no one else there except his assistant coaches and the players of the UK tennis team. We were sort of out of sight because we were at the edge of the bleachers in the boiler room doing our workout, but we couldn't help but watch around the corner, and we got to see Dan Issel and Mike Pratt practice. We were thrilled to see the Wildcats train and, of course, hear the comments by Coach Rupp. After the UK basketball team finished their practice, we had a temporary rubber mat tennis court that we would roll out on the basketball floor after 9 o'clock. We could practice tennis on the basketball floor until close to midnight, and then we had to take it all down, roll it back up, and put it back under the bleachers. Then we walked back to the Kirwan Complex where we all lived.

I also enjoyed running around the concourse. They had the glass exhibits with pictures and trophies and plaques, and I would try to read them all and learn about the UK athletics history. They had the basketball team pictures from about 1910, and they also had pictures of things like the Sugar Bowl that was won by UK Football Coach "Bear" Bryant with the quarterback Babe Parilli. Coach Bryant left UK and became the historic coach at Alabama. I was also very impressed with the names that were listed as the veterans of World War II from Kentucky that had been killed. I would try to read all of the names that were on that list as I would run the concourse and come back for another lap.

Jim Host

Founder of national sports marketing company Host Communications, first executive director of the Lexington Center Corporation (which built Rupp Arena), a multitude of other athletic, business, political, and charitable activities and recognitions

I first saw Memorial Coliseum in December 1954 when I attended the University of Kentucky Invitational Tournament (UKIT). LaSalle, led by the great Tom Gola, was defeated by the Cats — led by Cliff Hagan and Frank Ramsey. UK went on to have the only undefeated team in UK Men's Basketball history. UK rejected an invitation to the NCAA Tournament when the NCAA ruled Hagan and Ramsey ineligible because they were playing in their 5th year of academics at UK. LaSalle would go on to win the NCAA championship.

The next time I was in awe of this huge facility was when I walked out on the floor as the second fully-signed scholarship athlete in baseball in UK history. Coach Rupp taught a course in understanding basketball, which I took in my freshman year in the fall of 1955.

I was able to join the WBKY radio sports crew (the UK on-campus radio station) to do games in the winter of 1956. The crowds seemed so loud and close to the floor. Then, experiencing the 1958 NCAA Regional tournament at the Coliseum, and watching the Cats from press row win the tournament to advance to the championship tournament in Louisville, was an even bigger thrill.

Watching high school state tournament games enhanced the thrill of being in this massive facility in the '50s. In those years, it was the largest on-campus arena in the country.

Jake Karnes

The first director of UK's Disability Resource Center, serving in that role for forty-four years

Years ago, I met an elderly lady from Richmond, Kentucky. When she learned that I was a University of Kentucky employee, she inquired if I was ever inside Memorial Coliseum. After my affirmative answer, she asked if I had seen the soldiers' names on the corridor walls. I said yes. Then, with a smile on her face she informed me that her son's name was on the wall under Madison County and added, "Go look and see it the next time you are there." It was obvious this tribute to her son and other fallen soldiers had a very special meaning to her.

A swimming pool was part of the Coliseum until a new aquatic center was constructed on South Campus in 1989. The Coliseum pool was used for recreation and physical education classes. About 1970, there was a Donovan student (a program for students over sixty-five) and former Ziegfeld performer who enjoyed swimming. Although the college students considered her elderly, she was trim and physically fit, and enjoyed socializing with the young students. One day at the pool she dived off the high board and disappeared into the water. Where was she? Not in the deep water under the diving board nor at the deep end ladder. Shortly, her gray head bobbed up at the shallow end of the pool. She had swam underwater the length of the pool!

In 1965, President Lyndon Johnson was presented an honorary degree and spoke at the University Centennial Convocation at Memorial Coliseum. This same week the University was hosting a track meet under the supervision of Bernard "Skeeter" Johnson, director of campus recreation. On the day of the meet, one of the track meet workers burst into the Coliseum in the presence of the president's security team with a starting pistol in hand shouting, "Where is Johnson?!" He was quickly disarmed.

George Fletcher

UK basketball team manager of 1978 NCAA Champions, attorney

I was a student manager for Coach Joe B. Hall from 1978-1981. As a child and prior to becoming a manager, there was always an anticipation before Coach Rupp, and later Coach Hall, and the players emerged from the tunnel onto the floor to the UK fight song. There was this mystique of the operations behind the tunnel. Of course, the mystique was founded on the twenty-six years of amazing memories created on that floor. I was in awe of it, and felt like an excited kid seeing the nail in the floor where Vernon Hatton made the 47-footer to send UK and Temple into a second overtime in 1957.

During quiet times, I would move around to different seats in the gym and the "Crow's Nest" above one end zone, which people thought were poor seats back then. Compared to the top row of Rupp Arena, the "Crow's Nest" felt like mid-lower arena at Rupp. Bill Keightley told me this was the best, most sound basketball court he had ever walked on.

As a young college student, I didn't fully appreciate the symbolism of the "Memorial" part of the building at first. However, after I spent some time in the concourse during those quieter times looking at the names of Kentuckians who lost their lives in WWII and the Korean War, it quickly became evident that this place was much more than a basketball arena.

Jamie Vaught

Longtime Kentucky sportswriter, author of six books about UK basketball

My first real experience with the Wildcats took place in March of 1966 when I was ten years old. My brother-in-law (now deceased), a former high school basketball coach who was nearly twenty years older than me, and a friend had taken me to Lexington to see top-ranked UK play Tulane in the last game of the regular season. It was the year of the famous Rupp's Runts squad. I was excited and we had good seats – about fifteen rows from the floor. It was the first UK basketball game that I had ever seen in person. While the UK freshmen team played in a preliminary game, we recognized four Wildcat varsity players – Pat Riley, Louie Dampier, Tom Kron and Tommy Porter – sitting in the stands. I brought my twenty-five-cent game program and politely asked for their autographs. They obliged and Kentucky later won the game, whipping the Green Wave by a score of 103-74 before an overflow crowd of 12,000. Dampier, Kron, and Riley were the top scorers, scoring at least twenty points. We obviously came home happy.

And the Wildcats were the talk of the nation that week. Coach Adolph Rupp's team was having a sensational year, despite having a small lineup which featured a six-foot-five sophomore center by the name of Thad Jaracz, who had sixteen points against Tulane. Sports Illustrated, in its March 7, 1966, issue, featured Rupp and the Wildcats in a cover story written by legendary sportswriter Frank Deford. Needless to say, it was a very exciting time in the Big Blue Nation and I began to follow the Cats more religiously as a young fan.

Occasionally, my parents and I would get the unclaimed student tickets at Memorial Coliseum just a few hours before the tipoff during the late 1960s. We saw several games in person. I can remember Coach Adolph Rupp sat on the bench before a conference game with Mississippi State as he watched Dan Issel, Mike Pratt, and Mike Casey warm up. The three Issel-Pratt teams were really good, compiling a rather impressive overall record of 71-12, a winning percentage of nearly eighty-six, along with three SEC titles. That was another great memory.

When I was attending Somerset Community College (which was part of the UK system back then), my friend and I would often get student tickets to UK home games. I still can remember seeing All-American Kevin Grevey shooting downtown jumpers and famed broadcaster Dick Enberg sitting on the press row as he covered the game for the NBC network.

After some struggles in getting a media pass, I certainly remember my first game as a credentialed sportswriter in 1975 when Kentucky played Ole Miss at Memorial Coliseum. I was nineteen years old. As you can imagine, I was on cloud nine and had a very good seat on the hardwood floor. Writing for the campus newspaper at Somerset Community College, I actually covered a doubleheader, including a SCC-UK junior varsity game. In the preliminary game, it was neat to see football standout Derrick Ramsey getting twenty-seven points and twenty-one rebounds. In the varsity matchup, I remember then-freshman Jack Givens had a very good performance. He had twenty-six points and sixteen rebounds, both game-highs. I got to see Coach Joe B. Hall up close, and I was certainly starstruck. That night is something that I will never forget. It was a great experience for a very young-looking and inexperienced sportswriter.

Chip Rupp

Grandson of Coach Adolph Rupp, former college basketball player, Lexington business owner

To say Memorial Coliseum is "special" to me is a great understatement. My earliest memory of Memorial Coliseum dates back to the early 1970s. I would spend time in my grandfather's office before we would walk the grey, tile-lined hallway to the gym. There was a distinct echo in that hallway. It was almost like I could hear and feel the presence of the "greats" who had walked those halls many times in the past. On the way to the gym, we passed by the chain link "cage" where the equipment manager, Mr. Hukle, and later, Bill Keightley, made sure everything was in place for practice and games. As a student at Henry Clay High School, I played basketball in Memorial Coliseum on a few occasions. I felt as though I had a responsibility to give it my all to win and continue the success of those who preceded me. Memorial Coliseum made me feel like there was no way to lose!

Rob Bolton

Student manager of 1978 UK men's basketball NCAA champions, real estate agent

The first time I "saw" Memorial Coliseum was on the radio. Yep, it was Cawood Ledford's excellent voice in the late 1960s, painting exciting descriptions of the "scene," leaving indelible pictures of place and color and sound and smell. Not only was it a place of grandeur, simply and singularly, devoted to housing Kentucky basketball, but a place of raucous joy and winning!

The second time I saw Memorial Coliseum was from the top row in 1972, to see the "Super Kittens" (Conner, Flynn, Grevey, Guyette, Hale, Lochmueller, and Smith) play Florida. Dad and I went. I was fourteen. A JV team so popular, their games were separated from the evening varsity contest to let fans without tickets to the main event see the "Kittens" play. The place was full. Kentucky won, 108-64. Coach Rupp walked onto press row sometime after the start of the game to watch. The entire building stood and applauded for five minutes. He left before the game ended and again everyone stood cheering until he was out of sight. That day, I knew I belonged here.

The third time I saw Memorial Coliseum was as a basketball student manager from 1976-1979. It was now Kentucky's "practice place," as Rupp Arena was open. Truly a surreal experience when I stepped onto the hardwood the first time and bounced a ball! I could almost see my reflection in the glistening floor, with its lines looking as if they were inches deep beneath the varnish. Not only given a chance to stand on the famous "stage," but now a chance to live "backstage." A chance to experience the hallways, offices, training room, equipment cage, and locker room where so many greats shared time. The whole place sparkled! One could "eat off the floor." And the quiet, wow! Truly a place of basketball reverence!

By the way, Cawood had it right all along ....

Doug Flynn

Former Major League Baseball infielder and Gold Glove winner

As a young boy growing up in Lexington, Memorial Coliseum was bigger than life for a small kid who idolized Kentucky basketball players. Watching Cotton Nash, Terry Mobley, Larry Pursiful, and my favorite team, Rupp's Runts, still brings a big smile to my face. The building had its own smell, was always at capacity, and one could only dream of walking across its floors, let alone play competitively in this cathedral of basketball. My senior year of high school at Bryan Station, 1969, saw our gymnasium remodeled into a science wing, so I was fortunate to play a dozen games in the

Coliseum, including district and regional games. Little did I know that a year later I would be playing freshmen basketball with UK Hall of Famer Jim Andrews, Darryl Bishop (the first African American to suit up at UK), and scrimmaging against the number one varsity team in the nation that included Dan Issel and Mike Pratt. Include me on the list of folks who loved playing there, loved watching a game there, and still loves walking into this remarkable piece of Kentucky history.

Beau Robinson

Versatile radio personality, and UK sports "Blues Brother"

Midnight Madness at Memorial Coliseum was the most exciting night of the year outside of Christmas Eve for a young Kentucky basketball fan. Let the Midnight Special shine a light on me! The one night of the year that you could stay up late, past your bedtime, and watch the Kentucky Wildcats practice for the very first time. September to late October was Madness season, but the countdown started at the end of the previous season. The VCR was ready! I had my popcorn and was poised to watch the first glimpse of the Kentucky Wildcats. I always wanted to be there, but no way my parents would let me stay out that late. Not a chance. I had been to many games throughout the '80s and early '90s with my parents at Rupp. Madness was a bucket list item for me that seemed unattainable at a young age.

My first actual basketball moment in Memorial Coliseum was during the 1990 All 'A' Classic. The moment was painful, as a thirteen-year-old, to watch my high school team, Walton-Verona, lose in double overtime to Mayfield. That memory will stick with me. A bittersweet day. My high school team played in this legendary gymnasium, an accomplishment all Kentucky high basketball fans would be proud of. However, that accomplishment had been reduced to tears and a one-point heartache. Mayfield 69. Walton-Verona 68. It hurt.

October 31, 1992. Excellence was brewing with a team that was going to be anchored by the "MONSTER MASH," plus an outstanding freshman class awaited their moment to shine a few years later. This was going to be the night for me! For two months I begged Dad to take me to Midnight Madness, which was called "Big Boo Madness" that particular night. I pleaded with Mom to let us stay out late. I was on the straight and narrow. Studied hard. Stayed out of trouble at school. My one opportunity!

With approval from Mom, Dad and I made the drive from northern Kentucky to Lexington. A guy's day/night out on Halloween. It seemed like the hours lasted forever. We spent the day at Keeneland. The weather was an overcast, gloomy-and-gray cloud cover that smothered the Bluegrass. It was chilly. Keeneland has its own weather separate from other locations. It would rain, then get colder. Burgoo wasn't even going to warm you up for thirty minutes. As the hours slowly passed, the weather refused to improve.

Finally, we decided to go to Memorial Coliseum around 6 p.m. Fans would line up for days to get inside those doors first. The line meandered from the front of Memorial to Maxwell Street. It would rain, then it would snow, rain again, then sleet. More snow. An early bitter freeze crept its way into late fall. The weather was all over you like a Pitino full-court press! Night came quickly, and the UK students were ready to party on Halloween. There was no telling what I saw coming out of those houses on Maxwell. I started to sense that my dad did not want to be there. Finally, the line may have moved a foot around 10:30 p.m.

As we moved closer and closer to the front of Memorial, my big blue heart started racing. Kentucky! Halloween night! Although there was a chance that we would be cut off at the door with Memorial Coliseum being at capacity. 11:30 p.m. We made it inside the hallowed fortress of Memorial Coliseum. The new Kentucky basketball season was thirty minutes away! Coach Pitino already had the Big Blue Nation worked up in a frenzy after what he built the previous seasons. The clock was ticking down ... what is this in my seat? A Jamal Mashburn poster? You know the one! A souvenir button? A program? All the little "souvenirs" that I loved about Kentucky Basketball growing up.

Minutes and then seconds away! The time was right here and right now! Midnight, or slightly thereafter if I recall. "BIG BOO MADNESS" was upon us! A video of "Monster Mash" highlights played. Then a video with a mysterious figure in a cape who was playing an organ. However, a familiar and comforting voice said, "Welcome to Big Boo Madness." It was Cawood Ledford dressed up as Dracula and the crowd erupted in hysteria! Even the Wildcat mascot was in the Halloween mood.

Eight thousand rabid Kentucky fans lost their minds at the stroke of midnight to usher in a new season of Kentucky Basketball. As Jamal Mashburn and the Cats made their way from the crowd to the Coliseum floor, the excitement that Coach Pitino had built was at a fevered pitch. An All-American was leading the way for the Cats with a nucleus of upperclassmen and a very talented freshmen class.

When Jamal Mashburn and Coach Pitino were introduced, the crowd was deafening. I screamed, jumped up and down. I couldn't contain my enthusiasm. I may have pushed my dad, unaware of my surroundings. I was five years old again on Christmas morning ... just on Halloween night ... a very late night. For what seemed a brief moment in time, "Monster Mash" and company dazzled us with tricks and treats, now on November 1st. That late night/early morning set the tone for the rest of the season as we all know. This was Coach Pitino's most talented team at this point at Kentucky, and the rest of the college basketball world was immediately put on notice.

After an exhilarating day and night in Lexington, my dad and I made the trip back home to northern Kentucky. It was about 3 a.m. when we pulled in.

I was up a little earlier than Dad later on in the morning. As he came to the kitchen, Mom asked, "How was Big Boo Madness?" Dad replied, "It was a long Halloween. I will never go back again. Never."

I haven't missed a Madness since.

Tom Hammond

Lexington native, national sportscaster, member of multiple halls of fame including the Kentucky Sports Hall of Fame

I attended the first commencement held at the Coliseum in 1950, the year it opened. My grandfather, Thomas Poe Cooper, as dean of agriculture took part in the ceremony, and my mom and I sat in the stands. I remember what seemed to be the grandeur of the new building — the pomp of the ceremony and the varied colors of all the academic hoods. Being only six years old, my memories are limited, but I vividly recall that after the ceremony my grandfather introduced me to the commencement speaker, his friend John Sherman Cooper, who was then, I believe, U.S. Ambassador to the United Nations.

Years later, my wife Sheilagh and I visited then-Senator Cooper in Washington, and over lunch in the Senate dining room, he told many stories. He said my grandfather and he, who shared the same last name, often joked with people that they were related, though really they were not.

Walking through the new building in 1950, I was pleased to see a picture of my dad, Claude Hammond, a UK football player, on the wall of the concourse. My future father-in-law, Dave Rogan, a UK track star, was there as well.

Growing up I was lucky enough to witness some of the greatest games in Wildcat history at the Coliseum. The one season I'll never forget is '57-'58, the "Fiddlin' Five."

Vernon Hatton's miracle shot in the three-overtime win over Temple ... Jerry West and West Virginia handing the 'Cats a loss in the UKIT. (Nearly forty years later, Jerry would reminisce with me about his games at the Coliseum, including the time he broke his nose. Years later, improbably, a UK fan had handed him the old towel they had used to sop up the blood !!! It drew a great laugh and Jerry said, "Only a Kentucky fan." Later, I would be in the stands at Freedom Hall as the 'Cats won the NCAA championship.

As a member of the Lafayette High School team, I got to play many games at the Coliseum. You always felt you were in the big time when you played there with the college-level facilities and atmosphere. On Saturday mornings, several players from Lafayette and Henry Clay would sometimes sneak into the Coliseum for pickup games. We used an unlocked door at the rear of the building to get in. It was deserted except for the custodian, George, who looked the other way. George always swept the Coliseum floor at halftime of UK games. Of course, the state high school tournament was one of the Coliseum's most popular events each year it was held there.

Sometimes during the season I would somehow find my way to the equipment cage under the stands, in search of some UK gear. The equipment manager, Mr. Hukle, treated that equipment as if it were his own, even for the players. I think the only thing I ever got was a pair of socks. Years later, Bill Keightley was a little more liberal with the Wildcat gear.

As a UK student, I never missed a game, including those of my all-time favorite team, "Rupp's Runts." I was friends with many of the players and would often hang out with them. I had known my future broadcast partner Larry Conley since we were both sixteen, Thad Jaracz was a Lafayette teammate, Pat Riley had a summer job at a horse farm where I also worked, and Jim LeMaster was a fraternity brother. They passed the ball like no team I have seen before or since. I was in the stands and then the hotel with them after the landmark loss to Texas Western in the NCAA championship game in College Park, Maryland.

While we were students, we also went to the Coliseum for reasons other than basketball: class registration before each semester; concerts; lectures; an address by a sitting U.S. President, Lyndon Johnson; and even some closed-circuit telecasts of Muhammad Ali's heavyweight title fights. My graduation ceremonies for both high school and college were held at the Coliseum.

Much time after graduation was spent getting into the Coliseum without a basketball ticket (I had a few tricks up my sleeve), until I landed my first real job at WVLK radio, where I would sometimes be able to sit on press row. Occasionally, the opposing team would require an engineer to help originate their broadcast and would ask WVLK to supply one. I was no engineer, but once I learned that all you had to do was hook up a couple of wires and ride the controls, I volunteered for the job. I got paid to watch the game!!

My most important Memorial Coliseum memory is after I was hired at WLEX. The first event I did on television was play-by-play of a Kentucky rout of Kansas, led by Dan Issel and Mike Pratt, in December, 1969, the first step in an improbable career that would take me places I could never have dreamed.

My job at WLEX opened a new world as I was suddenly on a first-name basis with coaches, conducted many interviews, and became a regular at practices. (With Coach Rupp, no one ever said a word except him; you could hear the shoes squeak on the floor. Coach Pitino installed a speaker so nobody could miss his instructions.)

When NBC would come to town to do a UK game with Dick Enberg, Billy Packer, and Al McGuire, I would sit down with them and their crew to tell them anything that might help with the broadcast, making valuable contacts for later. NBC always parked the remote truck in front of the Coliseum and I remember walking by it and wondering if I would ever be in that situation. Little could I have guessed that I would eventually be on NBC with Enberg, with Packer, and with McGuire.

As men's basketball moved to Rupp Arena, I had fewer occasions to be at Memorial Coliseum, but through the years had plenty of thrills from women's basketball, volleyball, gymnastics, et al. I'm looking forward to the completion of the renovations, but, obviously, I'll always have a soft spot in my heart for the old building. All these years later, I still maintain that the original Memorial Coliseum, capacity 11,500, was the greatest place in the world to watch a basketball game.

Scott Cook

Former Oak Hill Academy assistant basketball coach, retired Air Force officer, author

In the Fall of 1983, I was a new college graduate, newlywed and essentially unemployed. Luckily, my wife had landed a full-time teaching position that paid the bills and allowed me ample free time to plan my future as a college basketball coach. Unfortunately, my alma mater, Asbury College, did not even field a varsity team at that time, offering me no exposure to coaching practices at the NCAA, or even the NAIA, level. "So," I asked myself, "why not learn from the best?"

I was a big Kentucky Wildcats fan and, being a naïve 22-year-old, wrote Coach Joe B. Hall a letter asking if he would allow me to watch pre-season practice. Unbelievably, I soon received a response saying he would allow that "on a limited basis." I felt like Charlie Bucket when he unwrapped the Golden Ticket.

For the next two weeks, I sat in the Memorial Coliseum stands with four or five high school coaches and watched UK practice. Like the others, I brought a notebook and pen to write down drills and other coaching tips for future use. Yet, I found myself so starstruck by Sam Bowie, Mel Turpin, Kenny Walker, and what was then-called "the greatest team ever assembled," that my pen was rarely engaged.

What I do recall was the thrill of a Memorial Coliseum backstage pass to view alley-oop dunks by James Blackmon, Coach Hall exhorting the team to run one more wind sprint "for Michael Jordan," and even a brief fight between Bowie and the feisty freshman, Winston Bennett. Bless Coach Hall for giving a young kid that opportunity.

Jack "Goose" Givens

UK basketball All-American, NCAA Champion, NBA athlete, and Wildcat radio broadcaster

I remember playing some games for Bryan Station High School in Memorial Coliseum. When we played other Lexington teams, like Henry Clay with James Lee, so many people in Lexington wanted to see great high school basketball that they had to move the games to the Coliseum.

A main memory I have of Memorial Coliseum is the final time we played there against Mississippi State. It was a historic game as we were about to move into Rupp Arena the next year. It was a struggle to win that final game. We were down several baskets late, and I thought maybe we had lost it. Then it seemed that all the history in the building, the great players of the past, and the basketball gods wouldn't let the last game in the Coliseum be a loss. It was one of those games where we stuck with it. I remember Reggie Warford playing great and we pulled it out. [Author's note: Givens hit a late tying shot to put the game into overtime, where Kentucky took the victory.]

University of Kentucky's Military Service

[Author's note: A special word of thanks to Allen Back, Lieutenant Colonel, U.S. Army (retired), who is the Recruiting Operations Officer of the University of Kentucky's Army ROTC Unit. He was very helpful in identifying and discussing the various UK campus sites, articles, and personalities discussed in this chapter.]

Memorial Coliseum is first and foremost a Kentucky military memorial. It preserves the memory of the thousands of sons and daughters of the Bluegrass State who gave the ultimate sacrifice for their country. The University of Kentucky is an appropriate site for such a monument because the school's history is firmly rooted in military service and observance. UK's very creation resulted from the nation's need for well-trained army officers in the wake of the American Civil War. From then to the current day, the University has supported and trained the nation's protectors of freedom.

The federal Morrill Act of 1865 provided states with land to develop or sale to create public colleges that would train students in military, mechanical, and agricultural skills. All male students enrolled in these "land-grant" schools were required to be members of the cadet corps (similar to ROTC units today), drilling and taking military classes along with their individual courses of specialized study. The purpose was to build a sufficient reserve of quality officer material for the country's future armed conflicts. Alumni Hall (later renamed Barker Hall) was built on the campus of Kentucky State College (which became UK) in 1901 as a multifunction facility. One wing of the hall was Buell Armory, where the cadets could march indoors.

Military Drill

This photo from the turn of the twentieth century shows cannon practice for the Kentucky State College cadet corps. Blanks are being fired from the school's grounds towards central Lexington to the north, while onlookers lounge on the grass in the foreground. Other observers sit atop the unfinished structure of Alumni Hall (now Barker Hall) in the background.

Spanish Cannon

Top: The city of Lexington gave Kentucky State College this Spanish cannon in 1903, perhaps as a testament to the school's military training program. It has rested on a pedestal in front of the Administration Building ever since. According to the UK archives, it was captured by American forces from the fort at Santiago, Cuba, during the Spanish-American War of 1898. This photo was taken in 2024, and Buell Armory can be seen directly behind it with its arched doorway.

The UK Armory

Bottom: Alumni Hall in the early 1900s, with the Buell Armory wing on its right side. A gymnasium wing is visible on the building's left side.

General Buell

Below, left and right: Two sides of a historical marker next to the Buell Armory wing of Barker Hall. The plaques give a brief history of the building, including its sections being named for Henry Stites Barker, an early school president, and Don Carlos Buell, a Union general in the American Civil War and a member of the school's board of trustees.

Buell was born in Lowell, Ohio, and graduated from West Point in 1841. In the Civil War, he commanded armies at the major battles of Shiloh and Perryville. After peace came to the nation, he moved to Kentucky and served as president of a company that dealt in iron and coal. In 1879 he was appointed by the governor of Kentucky as a trustee of the fledgling Agricultural and Mechanical College, the forerunner of the University of Kentucky. He held that position until his death in 1898, and was honored posthumously a few years later when the school named the armory wing of its new Alumni Hall (later renamed Barker Hall) after him.

UK in World War One

During The Great War, later known as World War One, the U.S. government established Military Technical Training units at schools across the country, including the University of Kentucky. Newly inducted soldiers learned skills such as construction, auto mechanics, and electrical wiring while still having time for plenty of marching.

Top: Soldiers stand in sharp formation in front of UK's Main Building. The training unit at UK was short lived, lasting only about six months until the war ended in November 1918. However, the global influenza pandemic struck Lexington during this period, and the gymnasium wing of Alumni Hall served as a convalescence clinic for soldiers.

Bottom: The gymnasium floor is crammed with beds for the sick, with a few even placed on the elevated running track. (Today, this wing serves as a dance studio, with the elevated track removed.)

Honoring Kentucky's Soldiers and Sailors

Top: The patriotic fervor on campus during and after the Great War ran deep. The engineering department commissioned a post-war plaque honoring the citizens of Kentucky who had served in the military. This ceremony to dedicate the tablet, mounted outside Mechanical Hall, took place in May 1920. The top of the plaque reads: "Dedicated to Kentucky Soldiers in World War by Students of the College of Engineering University of Kentucky, May 1920." Mechanical Hall was torn down in 1964, and the present location of the plaque is unknown.

A Memory Tree

American War Mothers was a national organization founded in 1917 as America entered the Great War. Its membership was open to mothers of men and women who had served in the military during times of conflict. Its mission was to support individual soldiers and sailors at home and abroad in a myriad of ways, all with a motherly touch, but appears to have become defunct in the early 2000s. In 1924, the Kentucky chapter of American War Mothers planted a memorial oak tree on the UK campus in recognition of the students who had died in the global war.

Bottom left: An embossed metal sign is set into the ground next to the memorial tree. It reads: "This Memorial Tree Planted by the Kentucky Chapter of the American War Mothers 1924."

Bottom right: The tree and sign are near the northern-most University entrance off Limestone [street]. The shield-shaped sign is directly behind the bicycle in the lower right of the image, with the memorial tree immediately to the left of the sign.

Memorial Hall

Top: After the Great War, the University began a state-wide fund drive to raise money for an appropriate memorial to the over 2,800 Kentucky men who had died in the fighting. Pledges stalled, but after nearly a decade of fundraising, planning, and construction, Memorial Hall was completed on the UK campus in 1929 as a World War memorial. In the photo, the beautiful church-like building nears completion. John Horine, a professor of Mechanical Engineering and an accomplished calligraphist, hand-lettered each and every name of the fatalities onto large sheets of paper, which were displayed in Memorial Hall.

Honor Rolls of Sacrifice

Bottom left: A memorial plaque is mounted beside Memorial Hall's front doors, dedicating it to Kentucky's World War One dead. Years later, a second world war finally came to an end with the United States and its allies again victorious. The federal War Department tasked each state with documenting its individual war dead. It was no easy endeavor, requiring painstaking inquiries and checks. Ezra Gillis, the UK registrar, headed Kentucky's accounting of the nearly ten thousand names of its war fatalities.

Bottom right: Gillis is pictured holding a chapter of the nation's roll of fallen heroes: *World War II Honor List of Dead and Missing: State of Kentucky*, dated June 1946. Professor Gillis likely had no idea at the time how the names of these heroic individuals would be incorporated within the structure of the University's long-planned field house.

Welcome Home

The conclusion of World War Two brought home many young Kentucky men that soon married and started families. Their military service qualified them for federal college funds under the new G.I. Bill. Across the nation, colleges and universities were forced to scramble to provide housing for the huge influx of married veterans. UK purchased hundreds of small, prefabricated war surplus buildings from the U.S. government as houses. These were assembled in a new neighborhood called Cooperstown, located at the then-southern edge of campus. The housing area was christened after Thomas Poe Cooper, dean of the College of Agriculture and Home Economics, and acting president of the University for a period during the war. The hastily erected community would allow UK to meet the educational aspirations of thousands of deserving veterans over the years.

Top: A view of Cooperstown's many tiny homes in March 1946. These were situated in what is now the modern dormitory quarter along Woodland Avenue near the William T. Young Library. An historical marker stands in this area to explain its past use.

Bottom: Veteran Doyt Bolling, aged twenty-nine, works a garden plot in front of Cooperstown houses while his wife and infant daughter look on. The scene is from May 1947, and the prefabricated buildings would last a decade before being replaced by a series of permanent apartment buildings. In turn, the Cooperstown apartments were demolished in 2012-13 to make way for multi-story student dormitories.

Air Force ROTC Building Fire

An infamous incident occurred at UK during the Vietnam War. On May 5, 1970, large student demonstrations were held on campus in protest of both the war in Southeast Asia and the recent killings of four students at Kent State University by panicked National Guardsman during similar war demonstrations. A large number of police officers from the University and Lexington forces, as well as state troopers, were guarding both Buell Armory and the Air Force ROTC headquarters in the face of threatening student crowds. Near midnight, flames suddenly leaped from the rear of the Air Force building, a one-story temporary structure at the corner of Harrison Avenue (now Martin Luther King jr. Boulevard) and Avenue of Champions. Firefighters could not save the structure from being gutted, and it was a total loss. The perpetrator, who had apparently used a Molotov cocktail, was never caught, although a female student was mistakenly arrested for arson. These charges were eventually dropped for lack of evidence. The Air Force cadets subsequently moved their headquarters to Buell Armory, sharing the premises with the Army ROTC battalion. Both ROTC units continue their proud traditions at the University of Kentucky today.

Top: A view of the aftermath of the fire from Harrison Avenue (Avenue of Champions is out of view to the left).

Bottom: The back of the damaged ROTC building is shown, with the old Blazer Hall rising above it in the background. A portion of the third floor of Blazer also sustained fire damage.

About the Author

Kevin Cook has degrees in engineering and American history. He lives in Nicholasville, Kentucky, and has worked as a naval officer, high school teacher, and a corporate sales representative. This is his third book.

Index

(The page numbers of images appear in italics.)